DATE DUE

ASIAN BAR AND RESTAURANT DESIGN

BY KIM INGLIS | PHOTOGRAPHY BY MASANO KAWANA

PERIPLUS EDITIONS
Singapore • Hong Kong • Indonesia

CONTENTS

NEW DIRECTIONS, NEW DESIGNS

Hospitality has always been high on the Asian agenda. Southeast Asia is renowned for its varied cuisines — coconut cream and chilli-infused curries, noodles and *nasi goreng*, seafood extravaganzas, fiery *sambals* and satays, and much more — many dispensed from roadside hawker stalls. Singapore is famous for its informal food courts, and Bangkok's street food is incomparable. Whatever the time of day, or night, delicious snacks and drinks are on hand.

However, food isn't only available in these low-cost, neighborhood eateries. Since the mid 1950s, the rise of the mid-level restaurant has been fairly consistent,

especially as other cuisines have been introduced to the region. But it is only in the last decade or so that very high-quality offerings — in food, service and décor — have burgeoned on to the Asian scene. The choice today is unprecedented, a trend that is global, as well as local. The days when a decent meal and a pleasant waiter sufficed are over. Entertaining out is now a lifestyle choice, and Asia's Food & Beverage sector has gone through the roof.

Even though this book comments on food and service (and all the restaurants, bars and clubs included are of a very high standard), the focus here is on design, décor, architecture and interiors. It is in this arena that Asia excels.

In a world of celebrity chefs, exorbitant wine prices, ingredients of superstar status and multi-million dollar hotels with flagship restaurants, the humble hostelry is a thing of the past. To be competitive, new restaurants need ambience, sex appeal, status and that certain *je ne sais quoi* as well as great food and service. These elements don't originate from the kitchen. Rather they are realized in the restaurant's décor and design — and it is in this area that Asia has come into its own.

Of course, social and economic factors are part and parcel of this rapid rise, as is the "design destination" trend that so appeals to the creative cognoscenti. However, something else, something much more fundamental, is at the heart of it. That something is what could be termed the "Asian aesthetic," an innate talent that has always been referenced in the region's craftsmen, but has now been given a free rein. Japan's top restaurant designers are currently in high demand in the USA and Europe, while architects and designers from Indonesia, Singapore, Malaysia and Thailand hone skills that meld Asian elements with Western technology. There's a strong international dialogue going on — albeit it with an Oriental slant.

It could be argued that the multi-kitchen restaurant is an Asian creation, as is the move away from the up-scale French or American white tablecloth and silver service model. There's a new informality in the dining experience, and it's interesting to see Asian wannabes cropping up in the West. In a reverse trend, many top American designers are attracted to the East — and are being employed to create new restaurants and bars in some of Asia's top hotels.

So what exactly are the ingredients of a hot, happening restaurant? What can we expect on the menu? Most agree that serious cachet is garnered with seriously original design: Big themes are passé, quality is key. And most designers are keen to emphasize that it is not just about the pretty picture; the operational logistics need to work too. Calvin Tsao of Tsao & McKown points out that when defining a public space, particularly a place of such active social interaction as a bar or restaurant, the design must address the fact that many of the same people will pass through the space at different times; it needs to look fresh and original during both day and night. Check out his multi-dimensional SynBar on pages 54–59.

Tsao goes on: "The high-style design concept with its big themes, such as big Buddhas or big circuses,

Above Brand new: Logos and branding are buzzwords of all cool eateries and a strong restaurant identity is a must in these competitive times. The entrance to this restaurant in Feast Village in Kuala Lumpur employs beautifully executed signage. Called MyThai, the elegant swirling metal motif is a celebration of the Thai noodle.

Opposite The top floor of the Dusit Thani Hotel in Bangkok is home to a high-end restaurant called D'Sens. As one exits the lift one is confronted by a super-luxe, Shirley Bassey-style antechamber, employing sophisticated lighting, materials and design.

inevitably becomes dated. A restaurant should aspire to provide a congenial environment where people interact. The décor should be rigorous and chic, but never upstage the diner."

An interesting point, concede the folks at Super Potato, Tokyo-based designers who started the trend for multi-dining venues with the groundbreaking mezza9 at Singapore's Grand Hyatt Hotel. That restaurant offers Chinese, Japanese, Western and multi-ethnic cuisine in a space loosely arranged around nine open show kitchens and counters. A spokesperson for the firm believes that restaurants are no longer about eating, but also about "enjoying the act itself." They provide an "experience." And at Super Potato, the designers strive to give their spaces a "new fertility as added value." What this really boils down to is restaurants with vision, energy and glamour.

Glamour has always been in high demand, but today's glamour differs from the aristocratic or hot Hollywood glamour of past eras. Nowadays, luxury has been re-defined as understated, serene and reflective, not in your face. The haute French restaurant with its over the top floral arrangements, chandeliers and flowing drapes may have signified the apogee of 20th-century fine dining, but in the new millennium it is giving way to something altogether more hard-edged. This does not necessarily mean pared-back contemporary interiors, although there are plenty of restaurants with bare walls, utilitarian materials and simple clean lines. Rather, it means a neo-classic or neo-vintage interpretation of yesterday's sumptuous, albeit rather starchy, spaces.

Michael Tan, the interior designer responsible for the boho-chic Scarlet Hotel whose Bold bar is featured on pages 180–183, endorses this view. "I believe that what we are seeing in restaurant and bar design today is an overlaying of more tactile and visually stimulating finishes, details and motifs, within thoroughly modern interiors," he says.

Alice Nguyen, an interior designer with her own prac-tice in Asia agrees: "The movement is away from the minimalism of the '90s," she declares. Previously with Hirsch Bedner Associates in Los Angeles, Nguyen pre-dicts more warmth and luxury in interiors. That doesn't mean Louis XIV furniture and over-the-top clutter, more a reveling in textures, saturated colors, luxurious fabrics — a look that embraces past forms and designs, but presents them in a new and sexy manner. See her Ink Club Bar on pages 238–243.

Left Sophisticated lighting and high quality materials are key to the well-designed restaurant. At Dragonfly in Jakarta, an asymmetric back-lit onyx high table, a gold-and-black lit panel and concealed spots in an overhead lamp made from old railway sleepers are imaginative and eye-catching.

Be that as it may, and there is dialogue enough on industry trends in magazines, on the internet and in countless tomes, it's interesting to look at *why* this leap has occurred in the hospitality industry. Certainly money seems to be no object as restaurateurs and hoteliers are spending more than ever before. And there is clearly no shortage of imagination in designs — and no shortage of innovative chefs. If, only ten years' ago, we were happy with tasty food, polite service and semi-pleasant surrounds, why do we demand so much more now?

Yuhkichi Kawai of Design Spirits, whose multi-ethnic, atmospheric Feast Village may be seen on pages 146–151, believes that the trend for more expense and more decoration is an example of the inexorable advance of capitalism, dryly commenting that only the Japanese Tea Master and John Pawson can "do" minimalism! Erik L'Heureux, an architect and interior designer based in New York who has also worked on spaces in Asia, cites globalization as the factor behind the growth of the high-design restaurant market. "As people become more traveled and more informed, they want more," he notes. "The restaurant experience is no longer just about food. It is an entire experience — atmosphere, ambience, food, service, and more." A case in point is his design for a dinner and dance venue in Singapore (see pages 244–247).

It also needs to be noted that this desire for stylish surrounds and high-end products isn't confined to the odd night out. Rather it is simply one aspect of what could be called "the advance of the lifestyle choice." Prosperity and globalization have brought an awareness of (and a desire for) beautiful things — in the home, in the office and on holiday. The 1990s' café scene in Barcelona, the launching of design magazine *Wallpaper* in 1996 and the phenomenal growth of the modern art market are all examples of the same trend. The creative classes have replaced the chattering classes — and style guides point them in the right direction.

In any case, whatever the look, whatever the price, one thing is for sure: There is now more variety than ever in the hospitality field. In Southeast Asia, there is the added bonus of location. Be it a boxy wood-and-white modernist cube in Bali's hills or a revamped mahogany-and-marble blast from the past in the metropolis, it is certainly more than a visual feast. This book aims to showcase that enormous range in all its manifestations. Hopefully, it gives top tips for fine drinking and dining, music and clubbing, too. Most importantly, it is a voice for many of the region's talented designers. Enjoy.

Right Impeccable finishing and state-of-the-art lighting techniques characterize the work of Japanese design firm Super Potato. The Grand Hyatt Jakarta's aptly named burgundy bar is a case in point.

Overleaf East meets West in the design of Gonbei in Kuala Lumpur. Here Japanese aesthetics are mixed with a strong modernity by Yuhkichi Kawai of Design Spirits.

BALI

DAVA & MARTINI CLUB

Located within the stunningly designed Cliffside Villas Complex on the western side of The Ritz-Carlton resort, Dava is more than a cool addition to Bali's dining scene. For a start, its architecture is breathtaking; secondly, its natural setting is mind-blowing. Along with the Martini Club, it acts as the central focal point of the complex, but interestingly, it almost dissolves into invisibility integrated as it is carefully into the surrounding landscape.

Water is the predominant element throughout the whole complex. Designer Koji Takeda realized the significance of this connection from the start: "Even from the skeleton stages, it was clear that the keyword of the project was water," he explains, "And the location and sequence of Dava with the hotel itself and the new villas was very important." Entrance is via a dedicated open-air reception "island" seemingly floating above a free-form pool; this, in turn, hovers above the expansive Indian Ocean. From here, a curving staircase leads down to Dava, its surrounding waterscapes — and to the villas below.

The experience of walking from the entrance, over water (as it were), then down the Zen-style steps to the restaurant, forms a sequence that is part and parcel of the whole Dava experience. As one descends, the roof of the restaurant — modeled on the shape of a petaled lotus — emerges almost through the water. With reflecting pools, soft pale stone, gently swaying stands of bamboo and a cool tranquility, it's no wonder the villas have operated at 95 percent occupancy since they opened in early 2005.

Once you enter Dava, the first thing you see is a stunning aquamarine glass bar made from thousands of tiny cast glass pieces carefully set on a stainless steel frame. Another similar bar is situated outside above a lotus-and-lily pond. If it is nighttime,

Right Blue chip credentials: The shiny blue bar (and its replica outside and below) is paired with a grey slate wall that is echoed from a similar wall at the complex entrance. The rough, textured composition, a traditional Balinese technique, acts as a natural buffer to separate the bar area from the outside.

LED lighting from below causes the bar tops to literally glow; if it is daytime, their shades vary from cornflower to sapphire, glinting in the sun and forming a whole with the seascape below. Designed by Seiki Torige, a Japanese glass artist based in Bali, they evoke a feeling more oceanic than topographic. You almost feel as if you are in water.

If the Martini Club is the aperitif, the restaurant is definitively the main course. Pale Javanese *wonosari* walls and pillars in curvilinear shapes combine with white marble floors and dark *sonokeling* wood to create a series of intimate seating booths. Custom-crafted cushioned seating fits into round low stone dividing walls to create sensuously curved nooks, while a number of private rooms are artworks in themselves. An Aussie chef serves "global eclectic cuisine" with fresh flavors predominantly from the sea in clean and creative arrangements.

And for dessert? Sit out on the ample terrace, indulge and drink in sea air and seascape in equal measure: Bali nights have never been so good.

Above Much of Dava's appeal comes from its extraordinary location within a landscape of exceptional natural and man-made beauty. Architects and interior design company Koji Takeda & Associates worked closely with the landscape designers M&N Environmental Planning Institute to fully integrate the architecture into the natural setting.

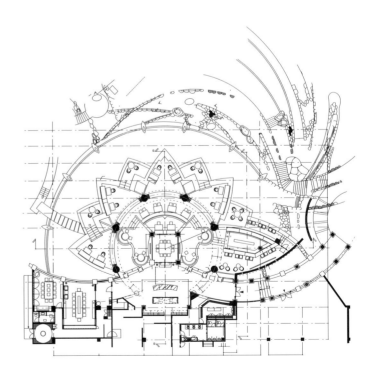

Left Kitchen counter: Sheathed in dark wood, the semi open-plan kitchen and adjacent wine cooler curve sensuously at the rear of the restaurant. Noosa Lighting Design of Tokyo was responsible for the unobtrusive, yet effective, lighting throughout.

Below Pillars of society: Six monolithic pillars (two seen here) delineate the central circle of Dava, within which lie a series of in-built seating booths upholstered in neutral grey. Above is a stunning skylight. All these semi-private eating enclosures are orchestrated to give panoramic views over the ocean.

Above Private dining rooms at Dava feature walls covered with hand-crafted sheathes using traditional techniques. Echoes from the bar include tableware from the Seiki Torige atelier and a palette of neutral ivory and dark woods.

Right Bali-based, Italian artist Philipos created this beautiffully grained artwork called "Loving Eye" as an outdoor decoration for Dava.

KU DE TA

Many meters of copy have been written about Ku De Ta since it opened on December 9th 2000. Dubbed Bali's first stand-alone, world-class eatery and entertainment center with design and victuals to match, it has become an institution in its own right. This is absolutely in order: Characterized by a drop-dead ocean-front setting, sleek design, fine Aussie-style food, slick service with 275 staff, and parties and events attended by every trendy "Yakker" (Seminyak resident), Ku De Ta fully deserves its high profile.

The architect was Fredo Taffin of Espace Concept, the contemporary tropical architecture specialists, with input from partners, I Made "Kadek" Wiranatha, Arthur Chondros, Guy Neale and Anaki Kotzamichalis. "Fredo's brief was to create an international, contemporary space that used the site to its best advantage, but would appeal to people from all over," explains Chondros. "We wanted it to be cutting-edge and cool, but also relaxed and laid-back."

Taffin, whose subsequent works include the Richmond Group's modernist The Residences in Phuket, the teak-and-limestone Villa Istana and Downtown Villas in Bali amongst others, rose to the challenge with a simple, no-nonsense approach. This makes sense when you consider the logistics: The 3,000-sq-m (0.7-acre) site sometimes has 2,000 plus people passing through it during the course of a single day; the kitchen is staffed 24/7; and meals and snacks are served from 8am to 3am continuously.

Built in the shape of a U, Ku De Ta's central pavilion-style structure is accessed by a dramatic curved stone staircase situated behind a fountain. An off-center column with the words ku dé ta are cubist carved by Richard North-Lewis, as are some other more abstract patterns on the staircase walls. Once up the stairs and in the main dining pavilion

Right The main event: In the main pavilion, the overall ethos is sleek and modern, with use of glass sliding doors, slate grey and deep rouge tones, and lounge lizard tunes from a sophisticated sound system.

beneath a wood-shingle roof, there is a view over an oblong pool, through a central court, to a lawn, beach and rolling waves beyond. Captured like a snapshot, the view is memorable at any time.

On either side of the court and radiating out from this central dining room are two further single-level structures in slate grey and deep rouge tones, with minimal decoration and flexible glass sliding doors. These house a second bar, a low-level lounge (which has a projected light show at night) and an open-air deck for tranquil breakfasts. Lining the beach

are two rows of custom-crafted, all-day loungers in clunky solid teak beneath deep red umbrellas: here, patrons are serviced from a 63-item grazing menu.

Within the main dining room, the atmosphere is slightly more formal. White cloth tables, a minimal stacked bamboo decorative installation on the ceiling and cute bamboo hanging lamps on the bar top provide the only distractions. And this is how it should be: After all, simply being at Ku De Ta is considered, by many, to be enough.

Opposite top Long water hyacinth tendrils tumble down from planter boxes on the flat roof, while tables and chairs spill out on to the patio for al fresco dining.

Opposite bottom A recycled teak and polished black glass bar features hanging lights with red-painted bamboo shades and a red backed, boxy display case for bottles.

Above A long corridor paved with flagstones leads to the restrooms; on the walls are some conceptual art pieces by Véronique Aonzo. Apart from these artworks, the only decoration is found in the nine squares logo of owner Chondros's company Nine Squares (see photo on previous page).

Above Nautical ease: Wooden boards, canvas covered blocky sofas and shade from solid umbrellas characterize the seaside deck. An outdoor shower with a large showerhead is a thoughtful addition for those coming straight from an early morning ocean dip.

Below As day gives way to dusk, patrons find that their daytime lougning has transposed to nighttime revelry: Umbrellas are under lit and tea lights flicker for a different atmosphere.

Above Watering hole at dusk: An oblong pool, surrounded by green lawns and a scattering of palm trees, juts out from the main pavilion towards the high rollers on Seminyak beach.

Opposite bottom The words "ku dé ta" are etched on a *palimanan* column at the entrance: Ku De Ta stands for "Kuta Denpasar Tabanan", not "coup d'etat", the owners are hasty to point out.

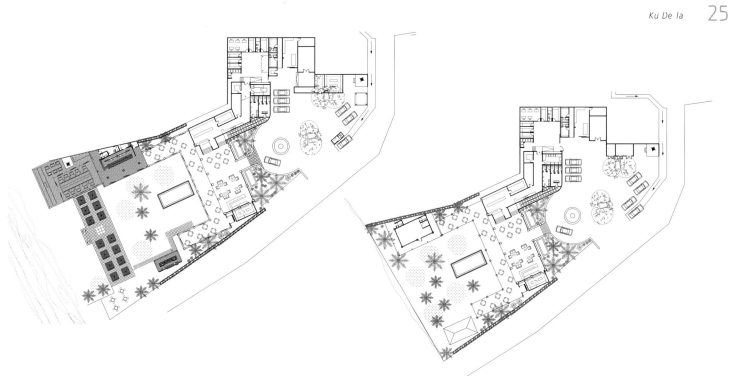

LAMAK

The owners of Lamak, a sizeable restaurant in Ubud, wanted something "a bit different." Say Yunita and Malik Prasetyohadi: "We didn't just want fabulous food; we wanted a memorable place in Bali too."

So who better to turn to than island design supremo, Made Wijaya? He, in turn, enlisted the cooperation of metal sculptor Pintor Sirait — and the result is an innovative garden restaurant with a show kitchen, outdoor bar and private air-conditioned dining section upstairs. Central to design details are the *lamak* or mats woven from coconut and banana leaf that one finds hanging from shrine altars in Bali.

"I have always loved the simple, bold, pre-Hindu motifs of *lamak*," explains Wijaya, "and we used these patterns as a leitmotif in the interior design." Predominant features include the huge, semi-circular staircase in stainless steel with wooden treads and a dramatic metal counter hugging the open-plan kitchen. Both were realized by Sirait and inspired by *lamak* designs. Similarly, Sirait's punched-out steel cladding and vibrant yellow semi-suspended shelves aside the small bar are sensual and curvy.

Lamak is accessed through a small off-street entrance where an inviting lounging area opens out into a leafy courtyard with the u-shaped building tucked round it. The cool court is enlivened by painted pool-blue, circular tables and wrought iron and wood chairs with comfy leather cushions, as well as plenty of tropical plants. Worthy of note are the downstairs restrooms: Funky heavy metal doors with working lights (red for occupied, green for vacant), classical colonial-era Dutch tiles and retro fittings revved up one reviewer to liken them to VIP lounges.

Softening the fairly rigid architecture are fluid asymmetric metal railings above wood slats on the upstairs enclosing balustrade. These are attractive from below, and double up as safety bars.

Right Lamak's central courtyard is anchored by an over-sized iron dish on a pedestal: this is a 19th-century molasses boiler from a sugar-cane plantation. Planted with palms and assorted potted tropical shrubs, it is a cool spot for a bite to eat.

Also upstairs is the enclosed dining area accessed through two huge cantilevered metal doors. Here, rattan loungers with *poleng* (black-and-white check) covered cushions and in-built seating make for a spacious area that may be hired for private functions.

Philosophy and aesthetics don't always make for happy bed-fellows, but, at Lamak, the trad/modern decorative scheme is central to what the restaurant stands for: *poleng* check, lights with scenes from the Ramayana, courtyard plantings and *lamak* motifs are combined with modernist sculptures, cool surfer dude photo-montages and clean lines, not unlike a microcosm of Bali, embracing as it does elements both ancient and new.

As Wijaya notes: "Bali modern need not be soulless. One can be contemporary and full-blooded, with cultural reference as well."

Above left Pintor Sirait is one of Indonesia's foremost metal artists with commissions that range the globe. His curvy bar front here echoes the adjacent kitchen counter front with sensuous shapes and motifs in metal.

Above middle Pendant metal lamps, from the Wijaya Classics range, were specifically chosen to complement the metal staircase. The over-large screen in the background features a scene from the end of a royal cremation — perfectly encapsulating Lamak's intention of showcasing Bali's ability to effortlessly mix the old with the new.

Above right Upstairs dining is breezy and cool, with great views of the court below. The calico cloth lampshades with woven *paku pipid* danglers are painted by Dewa Antara and feature scenes from the Ramayana.

Opposite top Buffer zone: The comfy colonial-style atechamber is cosy and inviting — and gives breathing space before entering the restaurant proper. The deep rattan lounger and cushions on the far side are upholstered with troppo print cloth from Sydney artist Bruce Goold (of Mambo fame).

Opposite bottom Private enterprise: Central Javan tiles on the floor, inset seating and bucket chairs with *poleng* check upholstery create a cool haven in the 22-seater private dining room on the second level.

Right Lamak's ethnic-modern signage is an exuberant graphic representation of the symbolism inherent in the design detailing throughout.

SPICE

The founder of the Hilton Hotel group, Conrad N Hilton (1887–1979) once famously remarked: "To accomplish big things, I am convinced you must first dream big dreams." In 1919, he bought his first hotel in Texas and, today, the group owns and/or operates in the region of 500.

The apogee of the group is the eponymous Conrad Hotels tier: offering top-of-the-grade service standards, drop-dead design, award-winning F & B outlets and premium recreational facilities in sundry sophisticated locations worldwide, they are the ultimate result of "Connie's big dreams." The Conrad Bali, which opened to much acclaim in 2004, describes its offering as "a complete lifestyle experience." I'm sure its founder would have been delighted — especially if he had sampled a meal at their signature restaurant, Spice.

Offering a "harlequin of ethnic cuisine, the best of Asia," the restaurant plays with spicy hues in the décor and combinations of local spices in its food. Housed in an oblong space beneath a soaring *alang-alang* roof, it has huge windows overlooking the hotel lagoon and the ocean beyond, as well as a sizeable outdoor dining terrace. The feeling is warm and inviting, with an abundant use of rich wood, tropical-natural coloured upholstery and roughly chiseled pillars. "The client requested something sexy and cosy," explains Teo Su Seam of interior design company Lim-Teo + Wilkes Design Works, Singapore, "As they use lots of spices in the food, we tried to blend that theme in with the interior décor scheme."

Directly in front of the restaurant entrance is a central lounging area with deep, comfy sofas — perfect for "sipping sherry — or a martini if you prefer!" says the hotel's PR Manager. On the right is the bar and entry to the kitchen, and on the far left a private dining room. Custom-crafted furniture from Bali-based Bika, some local fabrics and some from US manufacturer Pollack, coconut

Left With over 300 sq m (358 sq yards) of inside dining space and 160 sq m (190 sq yards) of outdoor terrace, Spice is large enough to seat 50 or so diners, but intimate enough for romantic dining à deux. With specially commissioned woven furniture designed by Lim-Teo + Wilkes, this is comfort dining at its most relaxed.

columns and teak walls, partitions and floors all contribute to the sensuous Asian feel. Sensitivity to site is evidenced by the layers of textures (yellows and greens from the surrounding landscape) in the upholstery and decorative wood-carvings inspired by the tribal art of the region. Similarly, hanging lanterns, constructed from linen and wood, were designed to simulate bamboo.

As the restaurant is only open at night, lighting by Project Lighting Design of Singapore is of paramount importance. With its dusky, mysterious atmosphere, Spice evokes all the exoticism of the East, yet still maintains a contemporary, rather than an ethnic, feel. This is a little like the hotel itself actually: low-rise and clean-lined, it is sleek and sophisticated, yet the beauty of Bali pervades throughout. Conrad Hilton would have approved.

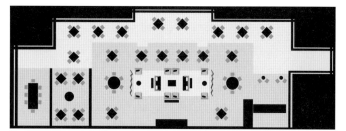

Top Giving uninterrupted vistas over the gardens, cascades and ocean, the terrace is simply an extension of the main dining room. Furniture, tableware and mats are the same as those used in the interior.

Opposite top left Pendant lanterns simulating bamboo and *alang-alang* thatching are ethnic features of this otherwise streamlined restaurant.

Opposite top right Slatted wooden screens, teak wood tables and chairs and tall unfinished wooden pillars all contribute to the warm, dusky atmosphere of Spice.

Right The private dining area features an impressive collection of tribal spears collected from throughout the Indonesian archipelago. Opposite is a line of polished bamboo that adds further privacy to the space.

THE WAVE

Love it or hate it, Kuta retains a rightful role at the epicenter of Bali's tourist scene. A base for surfers, beach bums, bikers and assorted Bali-based tropical dream seekers since the 1970s, its brash joie de vivre has proved resilient. Certainly, terrorist attacks have put more than a dent in its fortunes, but recent developments have seen it bounce back — and, rightly enough, this born-again babe is once more attracting the island's night owls.

One of the newer attractions — hogging a prime ocean-side seat — is The Wave at No 1 Kuta Beach. Inspired by the white, clapboard beach homes that dot the Caribbean, this cool venue is described by architect owners, Malaysian firm ArchiCentre as "a contemporary reworking of the time-honored colonial beach house." Comprising a three-in-one concept, with club/bar downstairs, open-air café on a terrace upstairs and an air-conditioned restaurant adjacent, it is a complete entertainment complex — with gorgeous views of blue rollers to boot.

Constructed predominantly from *palimanan* stone, the building is accessed via a wide curving staircase where an elevated white arrival deck with flying white sail roof leads into the club. Here, a 48-m (157-ft) horseshoe-shaped bar in Spanish arabescato marble with teakwood sidings is a great place to chill — while the adjacent dance floor comfortably accommodates parties for 200 or more. Upstairs, the clean, white 24-hour Coffee Bar is a modern take on a simplified retro pavilion. With its shell terrazzo bar counter and pebble washed floors, it's an inviting combo of California cool (think The Beach Boys' Good Vibrations and Surfin' USA) and modern Balinese *balé*. Really, it is a beach bar on an elevated deck.

Adjacent this open-air gem is Sailfin, a classy white restaurant with royal purple frills housed beneath soaring multiple roofs. If the coffee bar is the boat's deck, this is the heart of the craft. Floor-to-

Left A cosy corner with onyx fronted bar and lounging area sits adjacent the entrance to Sailfin, the upstairs fine dining restaurant. Ideal for pre-dinner cocktails, it breaks with the cool white-and-mauve color scheme of the restaurant.

ceiling glass windows offer panoramic views of Pantai Kuta and dreamy, pale mauve drapes offer both privacy and space. Food, naturally, emphasizes bounty from the sea and high-end cocktails and wines are served. This is a fine-dining venue, Kuta's first. And while you're waiting for your table, you are invited to sink into a warm sofa in front of a bar whose onyx front glows like the embers of a fire. If that doesn't make you feel good, I don't know what will.

For this project, ArchiCentre teamed up with interior designers Cicada Design, with whom it had worked in the past. Well known in Malaysia, the duo mainly focuses on residential projects, and this was their first foray in Bali. "We were trying to find a new modern way of expressing tropical architecture in an urban context," explains ArchiCentre's Dr Tan. From where I'm sitting — or from any angle actually — they've succeeded. The Wave is just what Kuta needs.

Above Deep purple: Pendant silk lamps and gauzy drapes in purple soften the white decorative scheme at Sailfin.

Right Bar stools in blond wood and steel from Teaktree House in Chiang Mai line the upstairs bar.

Opposite "Sailfin is a romantic, fine-dining restaurant where we hope there will be many first kisses, proposals for marriages, birthdays and first dates," laughs Dr Tan. Convivial certainly, but also clean-lined and design-savvy too.

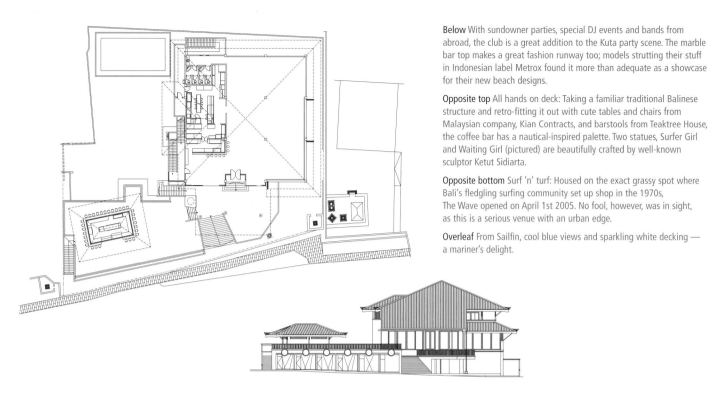

Below With sundowner parties, special DJ events and bands from abroad, the club is a great addition to the Kuta party scene. The marble bar top makes a great fashion runway too; models strutting their stuff in Indonesian label Metrox found it more than adequate as a showcase for their new beach designs.

Opposite top All hands on deck: Taking a familiar traditional Balinese structure and retro-fitting it out with cute tables and chairs from Malaysian company, Kian Contracts, and barstools from Teaktree House, the coffee bar has a nautical-inspired palette. Two statues, Surfer Girl and Waiting Girl (pictured) are beautifully crafted by well-known sculptor Ketut Sidiarta.

Opposite bottom Surf 'n' turf: Housed on the exact grassy spot where Bali's fledgling surfing community set up shop in the 1970s, The Wave opened on April 1st 2005. No fool, however, was in sight, as this is a serious venue with an urban edge.

Overleaf From Sailfin, cool blue views and sparkling white decking — a mariner's delight.

THE GREENHOUSE

Ubud, Bali's artistic heart, is no stranger to innovation and creativity. A stroll down its streets reveals elaborately carved temple buildings, cool eateries, humble lodgings and a plethora of galleries and craft shops selling innumerable goods ranging from trad tat to sublime sculptures and paintings. Indeed, it's well known as a haven for painters, sculptors, writers and more.

Nonetheless, apart from one or two exceptions outside the town center, Ubud's architecture has veered towards the traditional or the functional. That's just the way it's been. Until the GreenHouse came along, that is. A modern, linear, bright white construction, it literally springs out at you on Jalan Monkey Forest. Sporting the sort of bravura you'd find in Seminyak or Legian, its contemporary, curvy form makes it all the more unusual in Ubud.

Sitting aside (and owned by) the Pertiwi Resort & Spa, the GreenHouse is everything the resort is not. Pertiwi is all *alang-alang* and wood; the GreenHouse all glass and concrete. Pertiwi sits firmly in the "Balinese village" milieu; the GreenHouse employs a Western architectural language. Designed by Singaporean space planner Richard Sea, it takes its inspiration from greenhouses found in temperate climates.

The ground floor, encased in floor-to-ceiling glass sliding doors, houses a restaurant and bar, with a section for outdoor dining as well. As befits its name, the first thing you see on entering is a long steel-and-acrylic bar with translucent green PVC films lit with fluorescent tubes. In the evening it emits a striking green glow that is echoed by back-bar cabinets with a futuristic fern motif (also backlit). On the left is the conservatory-style restaurant in shades of grey and white with colorful green and orange hanging lanterns; on the right, a circular staircase leads up to the second level.

"I'm influenced by the Art Deco movement," says Sea, "where designs were based on simple lines, sleek function and form, and a simple elegance." This is particularly evident upstairs where more than a hint of tropical deco characterizes the air-conditioned party lounge and open-to-the-stars terrace. Retro day-beds, chaise-longues and a dark teak Chinoiserie buffet counter furnish the semi-supine indoor area, while the wide, semi-circular terrace and adjoining convention room are kept purposely clutter free. They can be customized for both indoor and outdoor meetings, weddings and house parties very easily.

Attention to detail throughout is evidenced by custom-crafted artworks and sculptures — modern interpretations of greenhouse flora — and ultra-smooth finishing. Pertiwi translates as "Mother Earth", so the GreenHouse focuses on nature and the environment both conceptually and in execution. Similarly, cuisine is of the fresh, green and unadulterated Pan-Asian variety.

Right Light, geometry of space and clean lines characterize the elegant exterior of this bright-and-white entertainment hub in Ubud.

Above Floor-to-ceiling glass windows give views out to the traditional Bali-style cottages of the Pertiwi resort. Large yucca plants and palms delineate the GreenHouse from its cottage-in-a-garden style sibling.

Left "I designed the flower bud pendant lamps to mimic the exotica in a greenhouse," says Sea. Using a Javanese wrought-ironmonger to fashion the iron frames, Sea handmade the amber tassels.

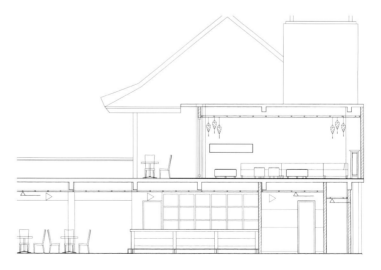

Above The upstairs lounge features low level seating and an orchid wall installation that runs the length of one wall. Orchid prints on PVC coated canvas mounted on wood are interspersed with solid sections covered in Shantung silk.

Below left The light-filled conservatory-style restaurant features high-backed chairs and tables designed by Sea and manufactured by a local furniture maker in Surabaya. Grey upholstered Sunbrella seat covers protect them from the sun's harsh rays. Adding to the tropical ambience are custom-designed and locally manufactured rattan sofas and armchairs around the perimeter. They are seen in more detail on opposite page at top.

Below right Natural history: A close-up of a fern — printed on film and mounted on to wooden and stainless steel cabinet door frames — is lit from inside using fluorescent tubes. The strong, horticultural motif matches the neon green bar perfectly. At night, the effect is particularly dramatic.

Above Lit from within at night, the GreenHouse has the vibe of a Miami beach bar or a Californian cocktail lounge. An outdoor eating section continues on left.

Top right The upstairs deck with umbrellas is a great spot for a party.

Bottom right Stairway to heaven: A floral-themed acrylic wall hanging may be seen through the glass in front of the circular staircase that leads to the upper level. At front, quirky cacti sculptures are carved from a one-of-a-kind stone composite material that is weatherproof, they were painted with a fine layer of glitter sealed on to the surface.

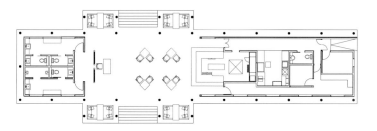

THE CLUBHOUSE

In many ways the super-chic Club at the Legian embodies the ideals of the Arts and Craft Movement: despite being built over a century after the movement's heyday and half way across the globe, it adheres to the principal tenets of renouncing superfluous ornament in favor of apparently simplistic designs, hand-crafted wherever possible using local methods and materials. The Movement's premier exponent, William Morris (1834–96), exhorted people to "have nothing that you do not know to be useful or believe to be beautiful."

This is apt when considering the Club, especially when assessing the freestanding clubhouse and adjacent pavilion that function as hotel reception, concierge, internet access room, bar, restaurant and poolside lounging area. A multi-functional space, it is characterized by clean lines, super sharp craftsmanship and a rationality that Morris would have approved of. There isn't a hint of clutter in sight.

The main building is an oblong-shaped, raised structure with a soaring *bengkerai* and *alang-alang* roof with a woven rattan underside: Open-sided, it gives uninterrupted views across a 35-m (115-ft) lap pool. Custom-crafted loungers line the pool, while a *balé* on left offers a shady, private space (see right). Eaters and drinkers can choose from a number of options: in the *balé*, at one of the modernist shell-inlaid wrap-around tables on low-level seating, or at a more traditional wicker-and-wood chair and table scenario. Another option is at the bar: made from white, green and brown translucent Indonesian shell pieces fixed to glass and back lit, it glows beautifully at night.

Apart from the shimmering shell ornamentation (which is of course functional as well as decorative), the only other embellishment is in the placement of perforated *banji* screens adjacent the al-fresco restaurant. Made from mahogany, their geometric shape is taken from the negative of an ancient basket weave pattern, and they allow for shadows and light to fall into the interior in different permutations at different times of the day. Conceptualized by design maestro Jaya Ibrahim (as was all the furniture) and incorporated into the architecture by Shinta Siregar, they take their cue from Eastern aesthetics, yet look curiously modern.

This could also be said about many of the objects produced during the zenith of the Arts and Crafts Movement: Keeping true to a sense of place with vernacular motifs and materials, their simple lines have encouraged periodic revivals and reproductions. Together with the principle of producing on a human scale, the movement is certainly relevant today. And in the case of the clubhouse, where Balinese materials and craftsmen were employed to creative effect, the parallel is obvious. While you sip a cocktail or check your email, you'll see that nothing is unnecessary, nothing ostentatious. Rather, all is restrained, calm, functional and beautiful.

Right At the Club at the Legian the poolside *balé* offers a secluded dining option away from the main clubhouse. Architect Shinta Siregar explains its clean, simple lines: "We didn't want to have any carvings in wood or stone, but wanted the beauty and richness of the materials to come through." She echoes the tenets of the Arts and Crafts Movement more than a century earlier.

Left Shelling out: Tables and bar counter were custom made by a local Balinese company in opalescent shell. The effect is shimmery chic, but practical too.

Below Lap of luxury: The long blue lap pool contrasts with the clubhouse's dark timbers and black terrazzo floors for sensuous light-and-dark effect.

Right: "The Club's initial concept was for guests to have total indulgence, in terms of service, atmosphere and facilities," says Shinta Siregar, and in the clubhouse, this vision is fully realized in its visual, elegant and understated drama.

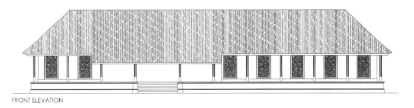

FRONT ELEVATION

Above middle No detail was left to chance either in sourcing or making objects for the Club at the Legian. Here, cute condiment pots are both aesthetic and carefully crafted.

Above far right Screen play: Siregar has always been interested in the screen as a decorative device and how light may filter through it. The detailed patterning of this *banji* screen is geometric and composed; it is also the only decorative element in the architecture.

Right The poolside pavilion is a relaxing spot during the evening for a bit to eat.

BANGKOK

SYNBAR

When this cocktail bar with move-to-the-groove sounds opened in 2005, Bangkok's nightlife was injected with a hefty dose of glamour. From the name (taken from "synergize" apparently, but it seems more than that to me), to the naughty-but-nice drinks and sophisticated décor, this is a bar that more than aptly accompanies the fairly recent renovation of the Nai Lert Park Hotel.

SynBar was designed by Calvin Tsao, a founding partner of New York-based Tsao & McKown Architects, as part of the total revamp of the former Hilton Hotel. In an interview with *The Nation*, a Bangkok daily, Tsao said that the renovation of the hotel was an exercise in "a quiet revolution." In other words, he wanted to modernize and update the interior design, but not completely annihilate what was there before.

This was a wise move as the hotel was particularly famed for its huge 3.5-ha (8.5-acre) landscaped garden situated bang in the middle of Bangkok. Originally designed by William Warren, amongst others, in conjunction with the hotel's owner who drew on her huge collection of plants, it is leafy, cool and colourful. SynBar, on the raised ground floor, has prime views of this abundant and beautifully lit jungle setting by night — and its curving glass frontage is an integral part of the bar.

Set off the lobby, SynBar is accessed via a raised, open-plan antechamber that acts as a stepping stone from the cool, minimal reception area to the hot-toned, sexy bar beyond. This area is overlooked by a spare stone sculpture executed by local artist Natee Utarit who is also responsible for the paintings in the all-day dining café below. Red and orange upholstered low-level seating, custom-designed mesh-like rattan chairs, teak coffee tables and small tables in fiberglass and automotive paint are accompanied by abstract amoeba-shaped patterns morphing and de-morphing on three double-sided plasma screens.

According to Tsao, the splashes of color here and in the other F & B outlets were deliberately implemented in areas off the lobby in order to create a "contemporary interpretation of mid-20th century modernism with an abstract sense of Oriental." Whether SynBar guests will absorb this is anyone's guess, but what they won't miss is the modernism once they enter the bar. Here a multi-colored LED-lighting system designed by Project Lighting Design in Singapore pumps neon hues over low-level circular couches, a bronze-trimmed bar, sexy Eero Aarnio bubble chairs suspended from the ceiling and a decent-sized dance floor. Fiber-optic "star" lights embedded in the chocolate brown carpet are alluring from below.

Carefully placed mirrors and deftly executed seating clusters make for intimate encounters. As a spokesperson for Tsao & McKown notes: "A properly placed mirror allows one to scan the scene in a discreet way, to 'see and be seen' and to peek, while the furniture promotes short and long term social interchange." What better arrangement for a sexy, nighttime bar?

Right The Eero Aarnio bubble chairs with silver cushions are eye-catching, not to mention comfy and sexy. Made from acrylic and chromed plate steel, the chair was designed in 1968 and gives the seated person a sense of privacy even in a room full of people. The American importer, Charles Stendig, named it the Bubble chair — and 60 years on it is an instantly recognizable classic.

Above and opposite below right One side of SynBar is sheathed in a bleached solid oak wood block whose texture becomes animated when the color-LED lighting changes.

Left The "circular bubble" motif is continued in the shape of the custom-crafted DJ booth, the stand alone seating, and the gently curving raised floor at the perimeter.

Opposite top A spokesperson at Tsao & McKown emphasises that their design philosophy as expressed at Nai Lert Park was "to merge, inside and out, architecture with landscape, to create synergy through blending the man-made with Nature." In this bar the garden estate may be viewed through one huge curving glass window, while within the effect is entirely and unashamedly urban.

Opposite below left Even though the bar is usually closed during the day, it can be hired for special events. When designing Synbar, the idea was to "create a feeling of light and space by day and a very different aura for the night." The masculine bar (partially pictured on right) is made from wood and clad with back-painted glass and bronze trimming; barstools have grey leather upholstery.

Above and opposite Pantone panorama: Set off the main lobby, this open-plan space next to SynBar's entrance is given a shot of color to celebrate the garden which envelops the whole area. In Iso restaurant below, there are splashes of lime and mint, whereas here the darker, sexy color scheme prepares guests for the club experience. The tall abstract stone sculpture is by Natee Utarit, one of Thailand's emerging artistic stars, who is better known for his paintings than sculptural forms.

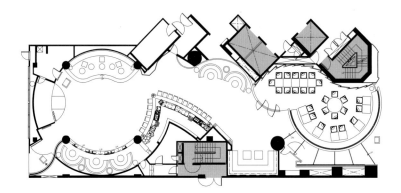

87 PLUS

87+ club/bar/restaurant is a truly international entertainment space. There is no Thai ethic, not a hint of Asian allure. Rather it contains a global food restaurant, a bar that boasts every cocktail you can imagine, a club that builds from mellow to cool to raging — and a design that straddles the globe with élan. 87+ would be equally at home on Sixth Avenue as on Sukhumvit Road.

In actual fact, it is situated just off Sukhumvit at 87 Wireless Road (hence the name) in All Season's Place, Bangkok's premier integrated office, retail, residential and hotel development. Its home is the hip Conrad Hotel, which also houses another establishment in this book (see pages 72–75).

Designed by local design powerhouse dwp cityspace, 87+ is a multi-functional space divided into three main areas: a restaurant called Italianate, a superior bar, and a nightclub. The overriding architectural and design device is the circle: Be it a curvaceous wall, a semi-circular space, a round dance floor, circular ironwork or swirling graphics and motifs on walls, doors and bar front, 87+ is a celebratory take on a contemporary roundhouse.

Separated from the bar by two curvy pivoting doors in steel, glass and padded luxe red cushioning, Italianate is a dramatic dining space. A custom-crafted, coffee-colored leather banquette lines the outer circular wall, while central tables dressed in cream and crimson restrict diners to a total of 35. Lowering the ceiling to maximize intimacy is a c-shaped, "fluffy" effect stainless steel chandelier with fiber optic night star lighting, while a custom-designed swirling carpet in earth tones and soft-upholstered chairs further the plush feel.

Earth and fire tones continue outside and into the bar and club itself. The bar area is characterized by dark wood tall tables and chairs, padded walls in the same fabric as upholstery, ceiling lights on circular tracks and a bar entirely clad in dark ebony. The bar front is in zany acrylic with slightly psychedelic, 3-d holograms; mood heightening and slightly disorientating, it's just the thing after you've had one too many! The only jarring feature here is the light stained wood floor: it could have done with being a shade or two darker.

In the evenings a sheer gold curtain is pulled back to integrate the circular club with the bar area. Seating is on raised platforms on either side of the dance floor: On the left are three rotund booths accessorized by ritzy sofas, low wooden tables with a rich grain, space-enlarging mirrors and an ironwork frieze in the foreground. On the right is a supine series of seating nooks with mock animal print poufs and a long leather sofa. Dynamic, swirling lights complete this up-market, nighttime scene superbly.

Right A dark, mysterious atmosphere is evoked at the entrance to 87+ where a curved wall in black leather conceals Italianate on the right, and a spray-painted metal-and-light installation guides on the left. The door itself is made from glass with signature circular graphic motifs.

Above The reception area features backlit shelves in fire tones to display bowls and pots in sculptural silhouette. Low sofas are ideal for reclining, while square glass tables with translucent laminated films make for an interesting glowing effect. Adjacent is a huge, walk-in wine cellar.

Left The Italian restaurant is lined by curtains made from a material that incorporates copper filings hanging behind a custom-made leather banquette. Up lighting brings out the fabric's metallic texture beautifully. Opposite is a staggered ebony and mirror panel wall.

Opposite top A metal grid, spray painted with automobile paint, gives access to private seating booths in the club section. Gold curtains, mirrors giving an illusion of more space, and ponyskin upholstery further contribute to the exclusive feel.

Opposite bottom Blast from the past: The bar is topped with stainless steel and clad in ebony, but the main focus is on the retro hologram-style graphics on its acrylic front. Constantly swirling, enlarging and dimishing, they change color too.

THOMPSON BAR & RESTAURANT

Despite objections from traditionalists that this restaurant is "too modern" in comparison to the traditional Thai style of Jim Thompson's house directly opposite, this is a restful dining space with a delightful color palette. Housed in a replica of the modular Thai-style home, albeit much larger and grander than its eponymous counterpart over the lily pond, it takes space that formerly housed the museum shop.

Up to 500 people routinely tramp through the famous silk weaver's former home each day, so extended facilities in retail, food and beverage make sense. Open-air café style dining is available on the deck adjacent the lily pond, while upstairs a large reception hall and clubby bar in colonial style gives a more traditional look. Below is the contemporary-styled, air-conditioned space designed by the James H W Thompson Foundation's Creative Director, Ou Baholyodhin, that is featured on these pages. It opened at the beginning of January 2005.

Thai-style aficionados would do well to look a little more carefully, as close inspection reveals that the airy space contains many modern interpretations of Jim Thompson's house and the traditional Thai house in general. One wall is given over to a mosaic of square concrete cast blocks, a reinterpretation but with the exact same mould of the original green ceramic glazed tiles on Mr Thompson's parapet. Another white tiled wall and a portion of the ceiling are slatted as if to represent his wood paneling. Windows along the canal side are in the shape traditionally found in Thai temples and old Ayutthyan houses, wider at the bottom and tapering towards the top. Again, they are copies from the original house. Concrete pillars are left roughly rendered to imitate the rough-hewn wooden pillars found in old Thai homes, while one wall of banquette seating features the ubiquitous Thai *maun kwan* (triangular cushion). Polished concrete tiles, the exact same ones as seen underneath the Jim Thompson house, ensure a seamless continuous flooring from the exterior into the interior.

Right The James H W Thompson Foundation is dedicated to "the conservation and dissemination of Thailand's rich cultural heritage", and this restaurant is a marvelous example of how ancient Thai traditions, motifs and materials can be reworked in contemporary forms. At the entrance, such touches are exemplified by the modernist lotus arrangement and the use of dark, polished furniture and semi-trad chairs with Thai silk cushions.

Above Cool oasis: On left of the minimalist bar, the window affords views of the somewhat wild and untamed garden planted with a lush variety of tropical ornamentals in the manner that Jim Thompson preferred. Thompson referred to his garden as "the jungle," and even today, it cools the site, while also affording diners restful green views from the large windows and doors.

Below The white tiled wall and ceiling, although traditional in form, was miniaturized by Baholyodhin to create a more refined, intricate pattern making it more suitable for interior usage. "The material is a high tech polymer resin," he explains "chosen for its light weight and strength, as well as its smooth, clean contemporary surface." In the background is a clean, spare lounging area with Balinese lanterns hanging above.

A delightful exposed concrete seating nook and bar is clean and spare, yet harmonious with the overall pale cool palette of grays and whites. Baholyodhin notes that this area is deliberately muted in order to "form a backdrop or canvas on to which the rich opulent silks from the Jim Thompson home furnishings' collection are displayed." Scatter silk cushions in a palette of burnt orange, sage green, pale grey and ochre are carefully chosen. The overall feeling is light, airy and spacious, as if to contrast with the dark wood and shadowy atmosphere of the adjacent museum home.

Baholyodhin sums up his design: "The purpose of this restaurant is to provide comfortable space for resting throughout the day, breakfast, morning coffees, lunch time dining or afternoon tea. The Museum House is the main attraction and I didn't want the bar and restaurant to be a distraction." Voilà.

Below and opposite top right This concrete cast wall was built so as to resemble a mosaic of the glazed breeze block tiles from the Jim Thompson house. Using pierce work, such blocks facilitated a flow of breeze and were found in traditional Chinese houses throughout the region. The polished concrete floor tiles are the exact some ones as found beneath Mr Thompson's former home; they are still in production today.

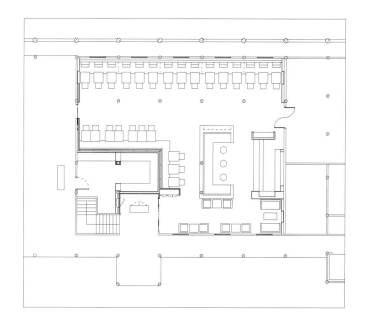

HU'U BAR & RESTAURANT

Named after a tiny atoll in Nusa Tengaara, Bangkok's Hu'u Bar and Restaurant is the third venue in the trio of Southeast Asia's Hu'u brand. Unfortunately, the first Hu'u, located in Singapore, has now closed, but the second in Bali is still a buzzing bar and bistro. The same can be said for this, the third in the series. A rare gem, it combines a sophisticated internationalism with a luxe, loungey feel and a real sense of place.

Owned by Singaporean lawyer-turned-restaurateur Terence Tan and Low Han-tzen, Hu'u occupies 743 sq m (8,000 sq ft) of premier space in the Ascott Sathorn. This is one of Bangkok's high-end luxury serviced apartment complexes, conveniently located near Silom and Sukhumvit in the Embassy district of the city. Hu'u complements its elegance in more ways than one.

Entirely designed by Colin Seah, the maestro at Ministry of Design studio in Singapore, the space was conceptualized as three distinct environments that are part of a single destination — bar, display kitchen and fine dining restaurant. The main focus is a stunning 8-m (24-ft) bronze bottle display installation that hangs from the ceiling above the bar. As the ceiling in this area is double height, it encompasses the space with a stark audacity. Lit from within, it is really a suspended sculpture — albeit with a practical function.

Downstairs, the lofty lounge space seats 120 patrons and acts as a lounge and tapas bar. Connected by a series of raised catwalk stairs and clear glass partitions, this leads on to a more formal 70-seat restaurant on a mezzanine level. Floors are of aged solid timber, and the furniture a mixture of custom-designed low leather sofas and richly toned Thai silk upholstered numbers. Dark leather feature walls and Thai, Burmese and Khmer art and artifacts — along with dramatic, moody lighting — give an exotic atmosphere.

Right A combo of stone, wood and metal forms the basis for the bar, whilst the over-sized bottle counter is made from welded metal hollow sections with lighting strips integrated therein. The result is extraordinarily dramatic.

Above Artworks from Low and Tan's private collection adorn the upper restaurant. "We wanted beautiful, aged and weathered accent pieces to add texture and dichotomy to the cleaner, more minimal lines within Hu'u," explains Tan. Behind the banquette seating is a line of such pieces: the central figure is 19th century of Burmese provenance.

Left "Hu'u really was set up as a place where people could just luxuriate in tranquil and relaxed surroundings and be themselves," explains Tan of his bar brand. *Time Out Bangkok* refers to the Bangkok venue as "the perfect place to deal, date, dance, drink or dine." Global cuisine, fine wines and a long cocktail list combine with an upscale urbanity in the design to appeal to an international clientele.

Opposite left Geometric forms and a dusky, sexy atmosphere are at the heart of the Hu'u design: Boxy lights hang above the bar.

Opposite middle The walkway to the dining room from the downstairs bar features underlit steps. At top is a gong acquired along the Thai-Burmese border.

Opposite right Modern plaster cast of a *bodhisattva* from Chiang Mai.

The restaurant upstairs is lighter and cleaner, with starched white table cloths, functional tables and chairs and walls that display changing artworks usually depicting Asian subjects. It is as opulently Oriental as its counterpart below, but altogether more dignified. Low and Tan's private collection of art includes both Burmese and Thai pieces and has been amassed over the years mainly from villages in north Thailand. Commenting on the artists' works, Tan says: "We wanted Hu'u to be a feast for the senses — touch, taste, sense, sight and sound."

Tan originally sprang to the collective consciousness as a partner in the original Hu'u bar adjacent the Singapore Art Museum, but he is also a partner in another restaurant group in Singapore and is totally committed to building the Hu'u brand laterally as a hospitality company that will include hotels, lifestyle, fashion and so on. Of his change in profession, he says: "Bars and restaurants are entities that I am passionate about, and having been in the trade for about ten years now, I still wake up and am excited about them." Passion being a requisite for a great product, Tan is sure to succeed in future ventures too.

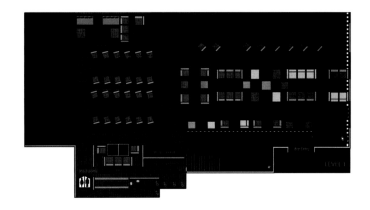

DRINKING TEA EATING RICE

This whimsically named restaurant brings to mind the refinement of a faultless *haiku*: its beautifully modulated interior, punctuated by quiet breathing spaces between sections, is as perfectly formed as this most sublime of Japanese poems. As each individual syllable counts in a *haiku*, so does each individual area in the restaurant. And when put together, the whole is equal to the sum of its parts.

The interior design was coordinated through the Singapore branch of the American company Wilson and Associates, as was the majority of the hotel. "The concept of the restaurant is really about the contrast of the crisp contemporary architecture of the room and the more fluid natural forms within," explains lead designer Michael Fiebrich. "We were striving to create something new and modern but completely Japanese."

Certainly the interior is calm and restful, with four tatami rooms, a sushi bar and teppanyaki counter interlaced with Western-style seating. Set on the third floor, it is delineated along one entire side by a huge, curvy glass window that overlooks the bamboo-and-beige lobby below. This allows the restaurant to be a part of the hotel, but also be *apart* from any frenetic proceedings therein.

"As the Japanese have a love of natural textures and their play on each other," says Fiebrich, "the material selection was very important for us here." Grey slate floors frame the entrance, but later give way to bamboo flooring, while bamboo is also used on all countertops. A river stone studded feature wall to emulate water lies behind the sushi counter, and further piles of such stones are placed at the entrance stairways to four private tatami rooms where they soften the linear steps.

Scattered throughout are a dozen or so oversized hammered bronze balls whose curvaceous forms further soften the interior, but also add a touch of humor. They vary in size from 30 cm (1 ft) to over a meter (3 ft) in diameter and appear scattered around the space like someone has dropped a bag of giant marbles. Also scattered on counter tops are a number of intertwined rattan sculptures; left to the imagination of the guest, they could be suggestive of the Thai *takraw*.

The restaurant's tagline is "Perfection in simplicity. Food as art, dining as contemplation, distilled to essence." Regardless of the cuisine (which is nevertheless pure and real), there is an attractive stillness about Drinking Tea, Eating Rice that remains with the diner long after the meal has ended. Be it the white gardenias in square glass vases by florist to the stars Sakul Intakul, the piles of pebbles, the light, unfussy woods, the unobtrusive lighting by Project Lighting Design — or a combination of all — the feeling is unconstrained, elemental and cosily sequestered. That's a rare feat just off the lobby of a 392-room, city center hotel.

Right An understated palette in neutrals, grays and light woods along with fluid forms and simple shapes contributes to the peaceful atmosphere inside Drinking Tea, Eating Rice. The central teppanyaki counter sits below a fluid bronze ceiling installation, while the sushi bar is semi-concealed by a glass wall in the rear.

Above The sushi bar lies at the rear of the restaurant. Natural materials, such as wood on the ceiling and bar and river stones on the rear wall, speak of Japanese sensibilities here.

Left One of four tatami rooms, this private dining room features chairs that are a fun take on trad tatami-room seating, a three-dimensional artwork woven from copper strands and fabric and tabletop items made in Thailand to a Japanese aesthetic. All artworks were sourced by Graphis Art, Sydney, Australia.

Opposite left Furniture was custom designed by Wilson and Associates and manufactured by Bangkok's Chime Design. Straight-backed chairs with grey upholstery surround square tables made of cherry wood in two finishes: natural in the center and ebonized at the edges for contrast. The teppanyaki counter, in foreground, is topped in bamboo.

Opposite right Switched-on lighting design is demonstrated by Wilson and Associates with these faux fish-trap light fixtures custom-crafted in bronze. "We took a simple element like a fish trap," says designer Michael Fiedrich, "and contemporized it into something new."

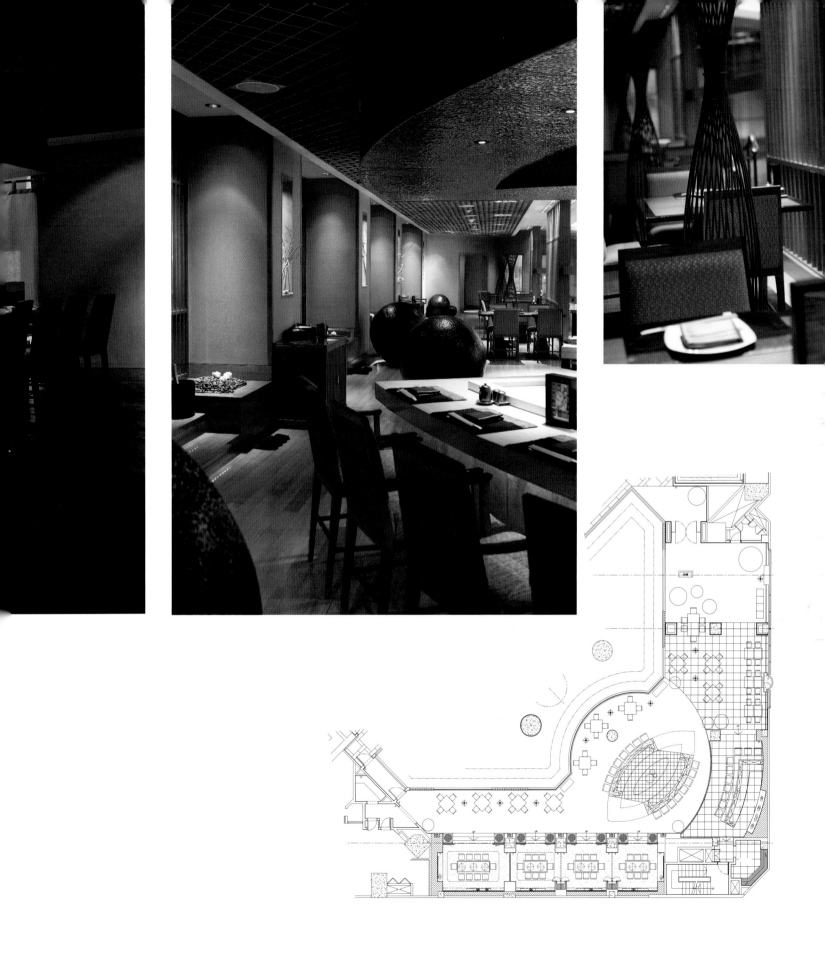

THE DOME AT STATE TOWER

State Tower in downtown Bangkok is a neo-classical monolith whose Italianate dome can be seen towering over lesser skyscrapers for miles around. All 65 floors of it are big and brash, but none more so than the top three that shelter beneath its cupola crown. Housing two restaurants and three bars in isolated splendor seemingly on the top of the world, it needs to be seen to be believed.

The journey begins at the tower's base, where a cavernous lobby leads you towards an ear-popping lift journey. A minute or so later, you exit into an antechamber with options: Ahead are glass doors leading to an elevated, open-air section; above is a sweeping double-sided staircase to take you one floor up to an indoor restaurant; on the right is a clubby bar. In addition, there's a vertiginous private party area. Most importantly, each venue takes full advantage of the view.

This is nothing short of spectacular. The faint-hearted are advised to remain indoors, because the al-fresco Italian restaurant Sirocco and attendant Sky Bar are accessed down a sweeping Spanish Steps type staircase that is heady at best, and disorientating and vertigo inducing at worst. Nonetheless, its sky-high mix of faux Florentine statuary and high-tech lighting, not to mention a bar base that changes color from neon blue to bright orange to pink, is uplifting and exhilarating. Perched 240 meters (787 feet) above sea level, another venue here is Flutes, reserved strictly for champagne imbibing.

The indoor venues are no less impressive. It isn't only the dining that has been elevated to an art form at Mezzaluna: Here the space has been conceptualized as an ancient villa, with double-height ceiling, a carpet that mimics patterns from fragments of Italian cloth, a central raised dais delineated by classical pillars and the ever-present view from a semi-circular floor-to-ceiling window. It's an open, airy restaurant in restful earth tones: blocky, backlit

Left The spherical Sky Bar with viewing platform behind is set on a broad wooden deck. Offering a near-360 degree panoramic cityscape view, it is not for the nervous.

onyx side tables and imported Chinese lanterns add exotica, while cool taupe, beige and cream tones are easy on the eye.

One floor down is Distil, an intimate space that, as the name suggests, specializes in different blends of whisky and is decorated in whisky tones. Whereas Mezzaluna is light and lofty, Distil is low-ceilinged, dark and sexy. Bottles on backlit shelves, an onyx bar with copper-toned, gold leaf front cladding, coffee-colored leather bar stools and retro armchairs are made for brotherly bonding. This is a masculine space, beneath a black painted ceiling.

"The original concept at the Dome complex," explains a designer from interiors firm dwp cityspace, "was to use a theme of earth, wind, fire and water. This related to the four zones of the horoscope and the owner's surname in Thai has links to the horoscope. Mezzaluna has earth tones, Distill is fiery, Sirocco brings to mind water, and the Sky Bar is airy." Neat, huh?

Above Aptly named after the wind that sweeps up across the Med from north Africa, Sirocco can be breezy and blowy. Extravagantly lit with fiberglass cupolas on pedestals and tall fiberglass tower lamps, it is a venue for power dining.

Above right Brotherly love: A masculine atmosphere permeates in Distil: classic 50s armchairs and bench seats in velour are arranged round onyx marble uplit coffee tables.

Above An interesting texture is achieved on this crescent-shaped wall with the use of randomly installed solid teak timber pieces and back-lit frosted acrylic panels. Situated below Mezzaluna, the pathway leads from the wine cellar to the lift lobby.

Opposite Reaching for the summit: Flanked by fountains and lit from below, the Spanish Steps style staircase is overshadowed by a neo-classical dome of extravagant proportions.

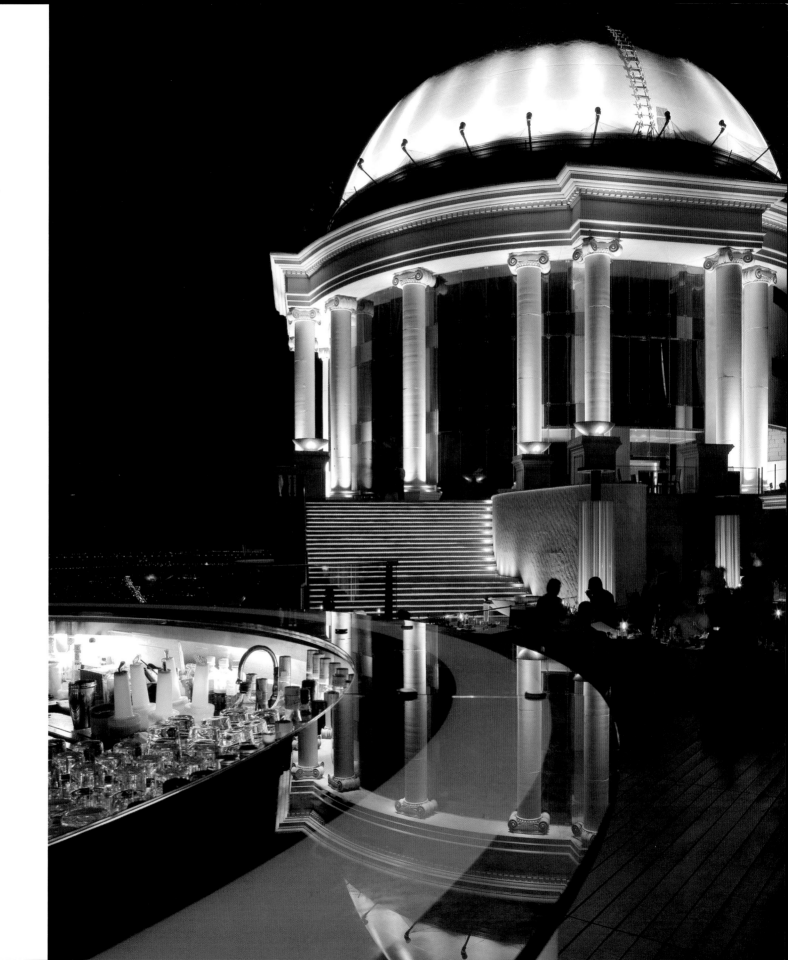

Opposite The staircase, with chrome-and-glass banisters and stained teak treads leads up to Mezzaluna, while double glass doors on below left open to reveal the al fresco Sirocco and Sky Bar. Below right is the lift lobby where the whole tongue-in-cheek pseudo Pompeii experience begins. Here, Italian mosaics inscribed with the owner's logo and a faux ceiling as if from an old villa set the scene.

Below The elegant Mezzaluna is light and airy by day, but dreamy and romantically lit by night. Imported Chinese chandeliers encased in cloth shades are quirky, while the dark wood bar has hanging lights in front.

Right, top and bottom Two more views of Sky Bar: Turquoise cocktail to match an acqua-lit bar front.

ERAWAN TEA ROOM

Adjacent the famous Erawan shrine, this new-style restaurant-cum-tea room is situated on the second floor of a plush boutique mall, literally one storey up from the site of the eponymous old tea room. That was housed in the Erawan Hotel, a veritable institution in the Bangkok of old: between 1953 and 1988 (when it was finally pulled down) the Erawan, and more specifically its sophisticated tea room, catered to all and sundry. Archives reveal that Marlon Brando, Richard Nixon and a host of other celebs passed through its wooden doors to pass the time of day.

The tea room's new incarnation is the product of Hong Kong-born, US-based designer Tony Chi. A sumptuous mix of highly polished wood, quality silks, memorabilia and more, it aims to recreate the nostalgic atmosphere of this bygone era — albeit with more than a nod to the new millennium. Commissioned and managed by the Grand Hyatt Erawan next door, the tea room is only one of the hotel's venues in the mall: above are futuristic meeting rooms and a residential spa — a radical concept in Bangkok.

The tea room itself is cluttered, unfussy, cool and sharp all at the same time. It seems to have one foot in the East and one in the West, a bit like its designer if truth be told. At the entrance is a retail section where ceramics, loose leaf teas, homemade condiments and other beautifully packaged and presented goodies are displayed on modern boxy shelves. Go through this section, and the room opens out into a series of seating clusters: Cambodian chairs and round or oval tables with opium matting tops are interspersed with a number of curvaceous, three-seat booths; Chi calls these conversation chairs — and certainly they are manna from heaven to the serious eavesdropper. Tradition and modernity sit well side by side here.

Right Intimate seating clusters are situated round tables with opium matting tabletops and sharp silver embossed feet. The menu caters for both short or long stays, with an imaginative tea and coffee list complemented by snacks and cakes as well as more substantial curries, noodles and the like. In addition, there are chess sets, magazine racks stuffed with newspapers and journals, and more.

The gently curving room is decked out in orange, gold and red hues, with Thai silk cushions, dark wood furniture and dark-stained wooden floors alleviated by a central cream carpet. Twenty-first century touches include a mosaic of stainless steel ceiling hanging lamps, Venetian blinds, large standing lamps with super-sensuous shades, as well as the streamlined, modernist display cases that reach up to the ceiling. These are countered by replica Indochinese furniture pieces, celadon plates, softly sensuous seating and an ambience with more than a touch of the exotic.

Slightly deco signage is reminiscent of Viennese Secession motifs: in fact the whole shebang brings to mind the Eastern equivalent of a coffee shop in Vienna (with the absence of tobacco smoke, of course). It isn't difficult to imagine artists, students, musicians and the like dropping by for a quick cup of coffee — and staying for three hours, or the whole evening.

Above The walls have been given a slatted wood feel, with grey paint going three quarters up and cream lightening the upper part. This design brings to mind the era of wood walled houses, the type of structures that would have predominated during the Erawan Tea Room's first incarnation. In fact, a collection of black and white prints of the old tea room and its inhabitants is hung here.

Left Retail therapy? The Erawan Tea Room opened in December 2004 to local acclaim; it has become *the* place for the city's chattering classes to buy gifts: never have antique Chinese teapots and loose leaf teas had it so good.

Opposite The deliciously curvy "conversation chairs" are a heady mix of plush red upholstery and super-sensuous shapes. Fitting snugly into their grooves are opium mat covered occasional tables with celadon tableware, while a blue plaid silk ceiling dotted with stainless steel pendant lamps sits above the 90-sq-m (108-sq-yard) space.

D'SENS

From the super-luxe, Shirley Bassey-style lobby to comfort-zone seating and an über-mod bar, D'Sens is revolutionary in more ways than one. Take its position for a start: situated on the 22nd floor of the Dusit Thani hotel with extravagant vistas over Lumpini Park, the setting is literally on top of the world.

Secondly, there's the food: D'Sens is the concept of Jacques and Laurent Pourcel, legendary twin brothers from Languedoc, whose Le Jardin des Sens in Montpellier has three Michelin stars. With other restaurants in France, as well as Tokyo and Shanghai, the brothers' particular brand of fine French fare with Mediterranean influences is justly celebrated.

As if that were not enough, there is the design. The Dusit Thani is one of the more trad-Thai hotels in Bangkok; Ayuthaya-style soaring motifs, glittering Thai silks and oodles of orchids are the norm in the rooms and the lobby. Yet the rooftop restaurant is almost totally European. With a cool beige, taupe and brown color palette, it is pared down, restrained and elegant. Designed by Imaad Rahmouni, a French architect of Algerian descent, it is intelligently restrained in order to give the views center stage. Yet materials are of an extremely high quality and the details are immaculate, ensuring the whole encapsulates an assured combo of proportion and glamour.

Rahmouni came of age (or at least to international fame) with his design of Vong in London, but he is also the interior architect of the Pourcel Brothers' other restaurants. He professes to adore Bangkok, explaining that, although the Pourcel venues are different, there is "a sort of spirit that runs through them all." According to the locale, he tries to utilize "the energy of the place by taking some tradition of the country" into the design. Here, he says the idea for the stainless steel topped bar supported by fish tanks was inspired by all the little aquariums he saw on the streets of Bangkok. Positioned at the entrance, and surrounded by a cluster of low round tables and chairs with a heavily cushioned sofa hugging a semi-circular window on the perimeter, it glows at night.

From this vantage point, the view stretches in one direction and the main body of the restaurant the other. It is l-shaped, with sleek banquettes in chocolate leather and cream-covered tables accompanied by modern interpretations of the rocking chair in chromed steel. Three semi-private circular seating booths are slightly elevated behind. Leather is the main interior design feature here: it covers seats, banquettes, the casing for the semi-private dining booths, and is even found on the floor. Some sections have a classic mock-croc imprint on the surface that contrasts with the modernity of the booth shapes. Red glows from boxy ceiling installations and a Paul Smith striped carpet luxuriates under foot.

Opposite In the entrance area more than 50 sq m (538 sq ft) of hand crafted colorful beads are used to decorate the walls (the total number of beads used is in excess of 130,000). Behind the desk a 6-m (18-ft) acrylic wall of embedded rose petals that was custom-made in France is not only beautiful to look at, but possibly brings reference to the Pourcel brothers' original restaurant, Le Jardin des Sens in Montpelier.

Above The bar is the best place to take in extraordinary night time views. Topped in stainless steel it is supported by two tanks each 5.5 m (16 ft) long containing 1,800 fish. Seating clusters sit before the bar: specially designed "rocking" armchairs are comfy for a post-prandial coffee or liqueur.

Opposite A restrained color palette and high quality materials characterize D'Sens. British designer Paul Smith allowed his friend Imaad Rahmouni to use his famous stripe design for the carpet, while boxy or circular panels designed and installed by French firm Barrisol make for softly glowing scarlet illumination from the ceiling. The red is picked up on the table decorations: triangular glass dishes with beads and a single gerbera on the dining tables, and a scarlet vase with a bunch of gerbera in the bar area.

Left and below left Attention to detail is evidenced in the specially designed silver salt and pepper pots, as well as European china and glassware of the highest quality. Even the floral displays of single gerbera stems were dictated by Rahmouni:

Below and opposite Three circular seating booths for semi-private dining are situated on the slightly elevated back section of the restaurant. Sheathed in leather dividers with a mock-croc imprint, they contain one of the three types of chairs that Rahmouni designed for D'Sens. The ones pictured here are of the regular variety, while rockers are found in the restaurant and swivel in the bar. All are superbly comfortable as are the banquettes and sofas.

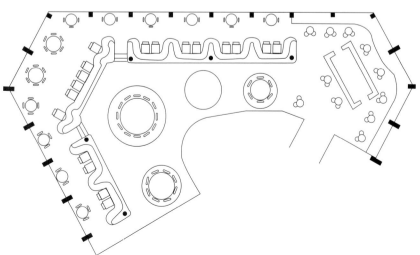

BED SUPPERCLUB

The brainchild of Sanya Souvanna Phouma and a number of partners, Bed Supperclub is in a league of its own — conceptually, architecturally and operationally. It is the kind of place that once visited is never forgotten. With its elevated cylindrical tunnel form, snappy interiors, high-tech sound-and-light system and an upscale clientele, it is unique. More importantly, on a wider scale, it is representative of Bangkok's increasingly outward-looking attitude.

There isn't a hint of Thai style here. Rather, it embraces a futuristic internationalism that would be equally at home in Europe or North America as Asia. Unsurprisingly, 3D computer modeling was used by Orbit Design Studio in the design stage, and the built form closely resembles that initially envisaged by its owners. Known collectively as "Bed Mates," they wanted "to provide a forum where people could meet, exchange ideas and feed off each other creatively in an atmosphere of style and innovation."

Using a modular construction method with a system of repeated steel ribs and concrete plank flooring, the entire frame perches off the ground on structural supports. This seems to make it hover above terra firma, an impression that is furthered by the external shallow stair ramp that gives access. In many ways the building seems more detached UFO pod, than attached eatery and club.

Nonetheless, as the name indicates, Bed Supperclub does indeed serve food, with a restaurant taking up 60 percent of the 800-sq-m (8,610 sq-ft) space and an adjacent bar/club comprising the remainder. Once inside, first impressions reveal a space that is smaller than it looks in photographs, but one that is carefully crafted and excellently maintained. Everything is pristine white on white with high-gloss white finishing, allowing for a blank canvas against which other senses are heightened.

This is achieved by pre-programmed, multi-colored lighting, a vibrant sound system, video projections of black-and-white films, high-quality food and drink, as well as "specials" in the form of parties, floorshows and the like. There is even a resident stylist to oversee proceedings.

It goes without saying that the venue has been extremely well received, attracting residents and tourists in equal measure. The combination of hip design, high-style interiors, seductive ambience, fine food, service and music has led to rumors of a second venue in Australia. Whether this happens or not is anyone's guess, as the Bed Mates remain tight-lipped on the subject. What is certain, though, is the continued success of this gleaming Bangkok venue.

Left Siam ease: Padded walls, upholstered "divan beds", modernist *khantoke* tray tables and soft cushions create an atmosphere as much dedicated to lounging as dining.

Above and right With its steel-clad exterior seemingly in the clouds, Bed Supperclub's structural supports remain firmly grounded on earth. Situated off Sukhumvit, Bed Supperclub is the brainchild of a coterie of Bangkok's creatives.

Opposite top Upstairs, Downstairs: Whether dining whilst reclining on the upper floor in supine style, or remaining upright on ground level, Bed has a seductively chic appeal.

Opposite bottom White on white is the theme here: Frangipani bloom in a curvy ball container, a select sound system and turntable for shows and events. In the adjacent club, silent films and videos are projected on the walls adding to the retro-futuristic feel.

JAKARTA

BURGUNDY

Le Corbusier's sweeping declaration that a successful space needs "a masterly, correct and magnificent play of masses brought together in light" is a pertinent starting point for an assessment of burgundy, the Grand Hyatt Jakarta's upmarket nightspot. For this super-streamlined bar and club is all about light. Even though it is also an assuredly conceived amalgamation of glass, steel and wood, it is the lighting effects, underpinned by modern clean lines, that give the space its drama and life. Without the light, it would be nothing.

Designed by Super Potato using a lighting design team from Daiko, this night-only venue is a wonderful example of how commercial lighting techniques have advanced in the past decade or two. Energy-saving and cost-saving appliances, fiber-optics and high output light-emitting diodes (LEDs) increasingly replace the humble light bulb — with results that truly trip the light fantastic. One of Daiko's major areas of focus, in addition to developing lighting equipment and systems that save energy and are environmentally friendly and creating pleasantly lit spaces, is to create "harmony between people, the environment and lighting." Take a look at the folks in burgundy on any given night, and see how it succeeds.

"The theme at burgundy is light," explains Norihiko Shinya of Super Potato. "The space consists of a variety of light impressions — such as plain light, streaked light, colored light and glittering light." Against a backdrop of deep red and luxe, are a number of eye-catching light fixtures: two metal-and-glass sculptural dividers "edge-lit" by a light box at their tips, a bar top that glows green and ghostly, color-lit ceiling panels, an illuminated central steel-and-glass see-through wine cellar and vodka freezer that reaches the ceiling and plenty of tea lights on tables. Optical effects are furthered by two striking glass walls that have been coated in a

Left A graphic pattern that is attributed to the abstract painter Victor Vasarely is here coated on to two glass walls to further a space defined by geometry. Planes and volumes in burgundy are rigidly horizontal or vertical, never curved.

Top High society: A long high table and benches for the sociable are lit by a sculptural light-and-glass "wall"; a second piece is located by the entrance.

Above Comfy bar stools upholstered in red line the glass bar which is both edge and front lit.

Above In order to allow the lighting to take center stage, Super Potato kept furniture, furnishings and materials very simple. The ceiling is painted a deep burgundy and the palm wood floor is stained black with a clear urethane finish.

translucent sticker with a geometric pattern conceived by the Hungarian-born French abstract painter Victor Vasarely.

The space, which is quite long and thin, is divided into three functional areas: a central space round the main bar with high seating, a lounge area behind the musical performance area and a rather out of place, clubby cigar corner. On one side runs a long communal high table in stained rosewood, while high seating is on custom-designed black or red upholstered swiveling bar stools with high backs and arms — quite the most comfortable bar stools I've ever encountered.

Super Potato is increasingly a global firm: burgundy was an early project, but more recently the Japanese design firm has gained acclaim for a London eatery and a Vegas casino restaurant. Its projects are varied in style, but unified by what Shinya calls a "new fertility as added value." As with le Corbusier's work, the venues are always masterly and never predictable.

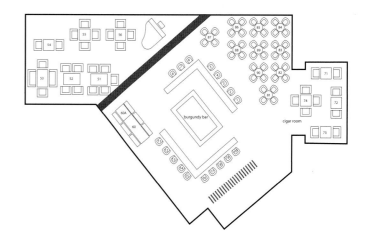

Top Making a decorative statement from a utilitarian object is one of Super Potato's design tricks. Here, the wine fridge and vodka freezer are eye catching, while a large light-box at the end of the bar doubles up as a table to display a wine cooler.

Above The far end of burgundy is slightly elevated, and high seating is replaced by clubby lounge chairs and low tables. Musicians occupy a space on right.

Top Recessed lighting in the ceiling and edge-lit glass panels provide the streaked lighting effects here.

Above For those who take their cigars seriously, a cigar corner is located at one end of the room.

C'S

"**The Hyatt group are** at the forefront of introducing new-style, innovative F & B outlets in their hotels," says the resident manager at Grand Hyatt Jakarta. "We started the trend for large, multi-kitchen, multi-cuisine restaurants with mezza9 in Singapore — and the rest is history."

Certainly, mezza9, the gleaming, nine-cuisine, multi-functional restaurant at the Grand Hyatt Singapore pushes the design envelope in more ways than one. Part theatre, part eatery, part light, part space, it was an instant hit when it opened in 2001. "A first for Asia," commented one magazine; "sensuality on a plate," enthused another. It was only natural, therefore, that Hyatt turned to the design firm behind mezza9, Tokyo-based Super Potato, for the equally innovative C's in Jakarta.

Smaller (830 sq-m or 993 sq-yards in total) and somewhat more restrained than mezza9, C's is nonetheless a masterpiece of design. As at mezza9, it overlooks the hotel lobby, so guests entering or exiting the hotel can look into the restaurant and vice versa. An open-plan, open-section restaurant, it boasts various food stations and kitchens as well as four private rooms. Food and beverages are used as decorative elements in themselves: Huge mortars and pestles with lemons, apples and oranges; big baskets of vegetables and spices; massive dim sum steaming baskets; and a steel-and-glass wine store with a large variety of wine bottles, are displayed throughout. The overall experience is of dining in a kitchen — but without the heat, noise, smell and mess.

Combine this with a variety of textures — Chinese granite, wood and water, mud-and-straw *tsuchikabe* walls, rough-hewn Javan teak finishes, back-lit dyed *washi* paper behind glass, a slate wall with flowing water — and the result is sensory overload. Geometric spaces are carefully decked out with innovative decorative elements in earthy tones. Animal print chair covers from a local supplier

Right Super Potato's design is a theatrical amalgamation of organic shapes and materials supported by geometric, contemporary lines. This is illustrated here at the entrance with the strong glass-and-steel wine fridge and fresh produce displayed in wooden barrels and bowls within.

Above One of the four private dining rooms embraces wood as its defining decorative material. Slatted wood allows diners some privacy without completely closing them off, while a smooth wooden table employs a lazy susan for ease of service. The central hanging lampshade is made from recyled paper.

come in a variety of colours; recycled paper lamps and bamboo stands on the deck are eco-friendly; custom-crafted tables have different shapes and permutations; table settings are multi-national with glass, ceramic and metal plates from Thailand, Japan and India, as well as innovative hand-blown glassware; and opaque, sand-blasted glass installations hanging from the ceiling above the chef's counters play on the letter C. Canapés, champagne, cranberry, culture, in fact 150 different foodie terms, are etched into the glass to outline the restaurant's core values.

At the restaurant's grand opening party on 14 February 2002, Jakarta was totally flooded. Access to the hotel was severely hampered by the deluge of rain, and members of staff were worried that people wouldn't make it. However, once the huge curtain was pulled back by Harry Pharsono, a local celebrity, Jakarta's elite turned up in their hundreds. A few years on, they keep coming: The restaurant is always packed.

Above Time-honoured Japanese techniques, such as traditional *tsuchikabe* (wattle and daub) and *washi* paper walls, give away the nationality of design team Super Potato. The back-lit *washi* paper that is shown here on the far wall was made with the help of a Japanese artist living in Bali. The main material is banana fiber, stained with the natural dye of curcuma amongst others.

Right A traditional wood-fired grill is used for grilling steaks, while extraction of food smells and smoke is hidden behind an oversized opaque glass hood.

Above A line of tables for two, with zebra-striped upholstery and views of the lobby, is situated at the right of the entrance.

Below "In both rooms and restaurants, we incorporate what the region has to offer — local materials such as seashell and coconut shells, elements from local cuisines, and more — in an up-market sort of way," explains the resident manager. This private room, called Coconut, is a case in point.

Above Details, such as the subtle change in the Java teak timber flooring as you enter the "outer" deck — it becomes more rough outside, more smooth and polished within — set this restaurant ahead of the competition. The outdoor effect is furthered by a slate wall with flowing water and a miniature Japanese-style "garden" with pebbles and a stand of bamboo.

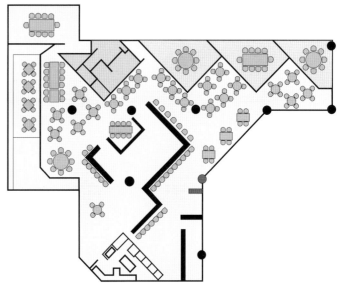

Above Roughly hewn stone and teak timbers follow the naturalistic theme.

Below Kitchen confidential: With woks and pots blazing and simmering, a compact central kitchen acts as a magnet for chef-watching. It is lined by counter-top seating and clusters of individual seating nooks. One hundred and fifty words (all beginning with C) are etched on to the clear glass extraction hood. The other parts are sand blasted to give an opaque effect.

CILANTRO

Owned by a prominent Jakartan family in the fast food business, Cilantro bills itself as the highest Asian bistro and lounge in Indonesia. Although this may sound a strange tagline, it isn't that odd as it focuses on the venue's greatest strength: its view. Situated on the 46th and 47th floors of a downtown building, Cilantro sports floor-to-ceiling windows and almost 360-degree panoramic vistas. On a clear day, one can see mountains on one side and the 1,000 islands in the Sea of Java on the other.

Sensibly enough, the interiors are of the pared-down, refined variety — allowing the views to take center stage. Light pours in from all sides, and this is welcomed in the high-ceilinged space. Tables and chairs are well spaced, further enhancing the open, airy feeling. With a main restaurant and three private dining rooms seating 300, and an upstairs lounge that comfortably accommodates 100, this is a large venue by any standards.

Cilantro opened in December 2003 in the premises that formerly housed the Jakarta American Club. Rather prominent geometric chandeliers that were on site at the time of the handover have unfortunately been retained, but these strike the only jarring note in an otherwise calm interior décor scheme. Designed predominantly by Fredella Nugroho, one of the family daughters, it is the family's first high-end restaurant.

"We wanted Cilantro to have a modern minimalist interior with just a touch of Asian influence," explains Ms Nugroho. "It had to be something more than just another Chinese restaurant," adds her brother Andrew, "so we offer Thai, Chinese and Japanese dishes, as well as high tea in the lounge."

In the restaurant, a clean palette permeates throughout. Dark chocolate, high backed leather chairs accompany mahogany tables with matte tabletops, and flatware and glassware is simple and

Left An elegant glass panel at the entrance sets the scene at Cilantro: in a beautiful aquamarine tone, it is echoed elsewhere in the spacious premises.

streamlined. A unifying theme comes in the form of hand-blown glass with the cilantro logo (two leaves of coriander) found in the door panels leading to the private rooms, at the entrance, and in front of the bar. Abstract artworks — colorful blocky oils with the use of gold leaf — by Irawan Karseno are another unifying factor.

The upstairs lounge, which is situated in the bullet point of this bullet-shaped building, seems to literally float above the city. Calm and restful, it sports comfortable, low sofas in olive, brown and deep mauve colors, as well as another glass-fronted bar and a small stage for a band. All in all, however, it is the emphasis on the real luxury of space that sets this venue apart: that, with views to die for.

Above At the entrance to the private rooms, a boxy floral arrangement sits at one end of the corridor.

Left Playing with panels in alternating solids and patterns, Irawan Karseno's works were specially commissioned by Andrew Nugroho for restaurant, lounge and private dining rooms. Originally from Surabaya, Jakarta-based Karseno is not only a prolific painter but is also very active as a consultant for corporate interior design.

Below left Going Japanese: At the far end of the restaurant, a sushi bar with stacked slate wall behind is clean and contemporary.

Below right A line of tables for four, with high-backed leather chairs and matte table tops, hugs the perimeter of Cilantro where enormous windows give fabulous views.

Above Light box: Shafts of light coming in from floor-to-ceiling windows and from glass chandeliers in boxy shapes that can be dimmed or brightened according to mood, ensure that Cilantro is airy and bright during the day and intimate and romantic at night. A sofa on left is a sensible addition for diners waiting for their dinner dates.

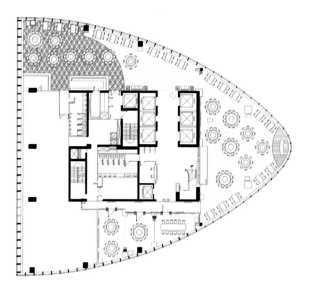

DRAGONFLY

As a dragonfly skims from pillar to post, so do clientele at this daring, dramatic venue buzz about from restaurant to bar to lounge. The current talk of the town, Dragonfly is the address à la mode for Jakarta's pretty young things.

This is quite right — as the interiors are theatrical, the service savvy and the food and drink aplenty. "Modern Asian" says the owner, Jakartan banker turned restaurateur, Christian Rijanto; "cutting-edge international" is my rejoinder.

The design here is of a standard that makes you want to jump for joy, imbued as it is with a lively creativity that is all the more impressive since the choice of materials is quite utilitarian. You would never guess that though, as the concept, finishing and considered details are sharp, slick and wildly imaginative. "We were lucky to be given a lot of freedom in the design," says Adelinah Rahardja of a2j design consultants, "and our contractor's contribution was very large — as he was willing to experiment and try something different."

Dragonfly comprises two main sections separated by a huge (7 m tall and 6 m wide or 21 x 18 ft) pivoting door, along with a small VIP room and two private dining rooms. Entrance is via a long, thin corridor with a natural liana installation on the left and an enormous lit panel partition with gold-and-black leaf motif on the right. The long walk heightens the sense of expectation which is fully realized when you enter the dining room. A cavernous space with a very high ceiling, it is dominated by a large-scale swirling fire "sculpture" that covers the far wall and curls round behind the bar.

The lounge/club/bar area is dominated by an asymmetrically placed central back-lit onyx high table. On stacked sleepers, it sports out-jutting sections that allow guests to sit both opposite and facing each other, across X-shapes as it were. With the glimmer from the counter top, the lit panel partition and two over-sized sculpted lamps (cheekily copied from Israeli lighting design company Aqua Creations!), this is a sexy space. A dance floor with parquet flooring completes the scene.

Choice accents unify the two spaces: a 9-m-long (28-ft) communal dining table has a tabletop carved leaf motif that echoes the pattern on the panel partition; old railway sleepers have been re-crafted with inset spotlights into hanging lamps; industrial floor hardener on the floors and black paint on the exposed ceiling flow through both rooms; and a semi-transparent, tall wine rack is accessible from either side. Indeed, the massive door that separates the two spaces can be pivoted on its hinge to fully open up the interior. With a flick of the wrist, one monumental, flowing space is created.

Right Playing with fire: "We wanted to have a real fire installation in the dining room," says Dragonfly's owner Christian Rijanto, "but in the end realized this wasn't possible for safety reasons." Nevertheless, the marmalade-toned, three-dimensional wall installation made from gypsum boards is dramatic enough to fire any imaginative mind.

Above A semi-transparent wine store divides the restaurant (pictured here) from the adjacent bar.

Above Close-up of the gold-and-black leaf motif on the panel partition. It conceptually unifies with an abstract carving of a butterfly on the pivoting door.

Above Double the volume: Paneled mirrors are placed at an angle behind the bar giving an illusion of extra space; they also pick up a reflection of the panel partition on the other side of the room.

Above One of the private dining rooms. Says the owner: "The ethos behind Dragonfly is simple: to deliver a modern reinterpretation of flavors of the east, while respecting the traditions of the past." Rijanto is quick to point out that the word "flavors" refers to both food and design.

Above High table: Running along the length of the rstaurant's bar is a back-lit, 9-m-long (26-ft) table with cut-out motif and carved, mock-cloth corners. It epitomizes Rijanto's vision for Dragonfly — "to create an eye-opener, something outside-the-box that separates us from the competition, yet gets us closer to our customers."

Left In direct opposition to the large dining room table that is placed parallel to the bar, a central high counter cuts diagonally across the space in the bar/club section. The two are unified, however, by the use of hanging railway sleeper illumination.

Opposite left and middle We played around with sense of scale at the entrance," explains architect, Sonny Sutanto, who also worked on the project. Full disclosure isn't revealed until one exits the long, narrow entrance corridor. It is lined by a huge panel partition, a section of which is shown here.

Opposite right An abstract carving of a butterfly is carved on the surface of both sides of the pivoting door — unifying conceptually with the leaf motif in the partition panel.

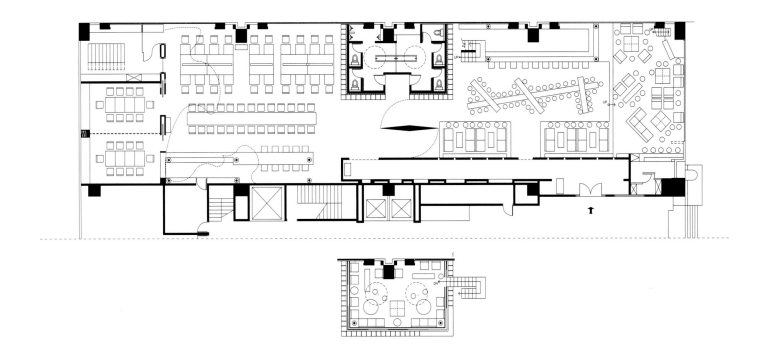

THE EDGE

Kemang Icon, a new boutique hotel in the Kemang area in South Jakarta, prides itself on offering an "urban lifestyle" experience. If that means high-end retail facilities, simple yet stylish dining, hot-wired business facilities, cool rooms and leisure offerings in the form of a spa, rooftop swimming pool and deck — it delivers on the promise. In fact, the hotel has everything you need for a stay in the city.

From the roadside, it isn't immediately obvious that Kemang Icon is a hotel. Boxy modernist architecture, a distinctive blue-glass façade and two lower levels sporting arty boutiques and galleries give the building more of a shop feel than a hostelry feel. You could be forgiven for thinking yourself in one of Kemang's more upscale malls. It's only after entering the building and focusing upwards that you realize that there is more to the structure than retail: A lift takes you up three floors to the lobby.

This "smoke-and-mirrors" introduction is entirely intentional as the owner/architect wanted to create something that was "multi-dimensional" and exploratory. "I was trying to get away from the rigid hospitality model," explains Sardjono Sani, "and give clients more choices than are found in traditional hotels." Certainly the 12 individually themed suites and rooms offer all you need for comfort, business and leisure, and the public facilities are more than ample.

The compact six-storey building is a mélange of hard lines, materials such as granite, onyx, metal and glass, and curvaceous forms sporting super-deluxe fabrics, flowing water and natural wood and plants. The whole is topped by a rooftop deck, complete with dining, swimming, lounging and spa-ing. Dining comes in the form of an intimate eatery aptly named The Edge. Offering both indoor and al-fresco dining — simple fresh cuisine in artfully natural surrounds — it echoes the overall ethos of the hotel.

Right Lap of luxury: A view from the lap pool deck back to the restaurant at night. A stepped section in the far corner can be used for romantic dining à deux beneath the stars, and is also used for musical performances from time to time.

When one exits the lift on the top floor, the indoor restaurant is ahead on the left, while a trellis on the right offers protection for outdoor dining poolside. A simple wood-and-white palette with acqua-blue frosted glass accents is suitably outdoorsy, and wooden decking is found both inside and out. A small bar and large glass sculpture by Seiki Torige separates the compact kitchen from diners, while floor-to-ceiling glass with Venetian blinds to minimize glare separates indoor from out. Large glossy Musa trees in

planters spread fronds over sofas with homespun cotton covers and gauzy drapes, all the while blurring boundaries between inside and out.

Whether you dine aside the frangipani-fringed pool, beneath a trellis of vines or within the restaurant itself, the atmosphere is airy, breezy and calm. Traffic noise is minimal and the vibe is more zen den than city gritty: it's difficult to believe you are in one of the most populous places on the planet.

Above The interior of The Edge is a play of light and space in the day, and more dramatic and alluring at night. Polished wood on the tables and wooden decking on the floors work well with soft cottons, plants and geometric lines.

Opposite top A small antechamber adjacent the lift serves as a waiting area for the restaurant. Simple in monochromatic tones, it is functional yet comfortable.

Opposite bottom Japanese glass artist, Seike Torige, conceptualised and crafted this edgy artwork in frosted glass. It sits adjacent the food counter in the restaurant.

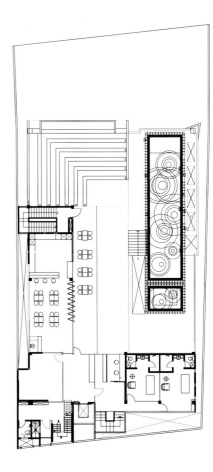

Above The entire rooftop at Kemang Icon is given over to recreation: Lounging and dining al fresco, swimming in the pool and on the top floor above the restaurant is the hotel spa and fitness facilities. Here one of the al-resco restaurant tables overlooks the pool.

Right A long mirror running the length of the slightly elevated pool reflects diners on the deck, and succeeds in making the space larger.

Opposite Furniture is cafe-style functional on the deck. It needs to be hard wearing in the hot, tropical climate.

LARA DJONGGRANG & LA BIHZAD BAR

Opened in August 2005, this unusual restaurant is part history, part cultural journey, part education, part myth. Straddling Jakarta's mayhem with a beguiling combination of old architecture, art and memorabilia, as well as a veritable smorgasbord of Indonesian cuisine, it is as varied as the city in which it finds itself. Indeed, a sojourn at its tables could be likened to a journey through Indonesia, even Asia, in its many incarnations.

Take the name, for example. It comes from the ancient Hindu temple complex of the same name at Prambanan in Central Java, where the myth of a young girl is celebrated. Revered as a symbol of filial piety, her story (and others like it) is increasingly being forgotten in modern-day Indonesia. In order to reverse this trend, the restaurant's owner Anhar Setjadibrata filled Lara Djonggrang with a treasure trove of artworks, thereby reminding patrons of the region's rich cultural and artistic history.

This is not a new trend with Setjadibrata. His Tugu Hotels in Bali and East Java and other restaurants in Jakarta are renowned for their extensive collections of art. Be it woodwork from a Chinese temple, ancient statuary from the Majapahit era, a serene Buddha image or a painting by a famous Indonesian artist, it has been painstakingly amassed over the decades by a determined collector. All credit, therefore, that it (along with countless others) is displayed for the public to enjoy.

"Many of these pieces would have been destroyed if I hadn't stepped in and bought them," explains Pak Anhar. The same could be said for the buildings themselves. Lara Djonggrang is housed in what was a semi-derelict residence that had been earmarked by the government for demolition; a meticulous renovation job, and the addition of courtyards and another structure at the rear, saved what is undeniably a piece of the city's architectural heritage.

Right Tuberoses and tiles, Moroccan hanging lanterns and elaborate woodwork characterize La Bihzad Bar. The beautiful long bar on right is flanked by portraits of Iranian kings who were patrons of Islamic Art. Oversized rice storage containers sit above the bar, while 150-year-old tiles are used on the floor.

The restaurant comprises a series of different dining rooms and bars loosely gathered round a cool courtyard space. The first hall is named China Blue, as its décor is a striking combination of deep turquoise walls and upholstery with scarlet accents in cushions, tabletops and curtains. Dominated by two huge Chinese gods carved from a single piece of wood, it is at once imposing and opulent. To one side is a singularly interesting private dining room dedicated to Indonesia's first president who was known to the Sedjadibrata family.

The Lara Djonggrang hall, complete with a statue of the goddess made by villagers in Central Java and a freize of *wayang kulit* puppets, has a rather more mysterious atmosphere, while La Bihzad Bar is dedicated to the 15th-century Herat artist Bihzad. Housed in a 300-year-old temple transferred from a small town in East Java, it features reproductions of work by Ustad Mohammad Saed Mashal, a 20th-century stylistic disciple of Bihzad, as well as portraits of previous patrons of Islamic Art.

Above Detail of a reproduction of a 1967 painting by Afghani artist Ustad Mohammad Saed Mashal on one of the walls in La Bihzad Bar. Originally painted on the outer wall of the Great Hall in Herat, but whitewashed by Taliban fanatics along with most of his work, it depicts the punishment of devils by King Solomon and the Queen of Sheba.

Above and opposite Not only is this restaurant a celebration of authentic recipes from around the archipelago, it is a rich repository of Indonesian art. In the Lara Djonggrang room, black walls are adorned with original Javanese paintings on glass, stone statuary doubles up as table bases, while center stage is given to an over-large statue of the goddess on her way to the heavens. Surrounded by a beautiful screen, it stands behind an ancient stone with inscriptions in old Javanese. The room is so arranged in order to remind people of the ancient legend. The story goes that the beautiful Lara Djonggrang turned down a marriage proposal from Bandung Bondowoso out of respect for her father, the king, who had previously been killed by her suitor. As a result she was cursed and turned into stone. However, the gods heard of her story, and she was invited to ride to the heavens on the back of a mythological Javanese lion. This room celebrates the goddess as a symbol of filial piety.

Left The atmospheric exterior of Lara Djonggrang is shaded by a venerable banyan tree and features over-sized statuary and tall wooden pillars decorated with oil lamps.

Below Ironwork pillars dating back to the Dutch era were used to underpin the ceilings in the China Blue hall. Painted a rich red hue, they accompany the turquoise-and-scarlet palette that is theatrically realized in the two huge Chinese god carvings. The long teak table, set upon a floor that is covered in Islamic tiles with geometric motifs, seats up to 20 diners.

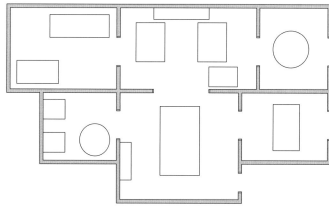

Above With its own private entrance, this room is a tribute to Indonesia's independence from the Dutch. Elaborate Chinese chairs with dragon arms cluster round a central table that ironically was once owned by sugar baron Oei Tiong Ham, while artworks and memorabilia donated by former president Megawati adorn the walls.

Below A huge Buddha image from Myanmar dominates this antechamber, while a pair of winged oryx on plinths guards the long table. A small bridge links this room with La Bihzad Bar and assorted courtyards behind.

THE NINE MUSES CLUB

Fine dining cognoscenti have an instinct for classic food/drink pairings, but what about food and music? Coffee and jazz, a barbecue and Blues, champagne and Chopin come to mind. They slot nicely together, but often the emphasis focuses on one rather than on the other. At a jazz club, the quality of the music may be fabulous, but the food leaves much to be desired; at an haute-cuisine restaurant, the piped music plays second fiddle to the dinner. Yet … surely it doesn't have to be like that, does it?

Not according to Gil D'Harcour, owner, designer, restaurant consultant and the brain behind the Nine Muses Club. Together with his partner, who runs the first and only independent Academy of Music with an international standard curriculum in Indonesia, and two other partners, he conceptualized, constructed and opened the club in 2004. Aiming to set the record straight on both the culinary and the music front, D'Harcour bills the venue as a "dining music club." Dishing up a potent combination of "fine food and service with a passion for music," it has more than a dash of high style too.

"The idea was to have a jazz club with serious musicians," says D'Harcour, "but if it was just the jazz, it wouldn't attract enough clientele. So we put serious work into the design and food — and we also organize events and private functions." Latin jazz, Dixieland, flamenco, French cabaret and even a 50-piece orchestra in the garden have been featured since its inception.

Music aside, the club attracts with an aesthetic appeal that is elegant, sensual — and playful. Housed in what was once a very ordinary suburban residence now entirely sheathed in lava stone, the patron is led on a journey of discovery from the entrance to the exit. First of all, a stupa above the front door and a cloistered corridor with a particularly fine Cambodian Buddha head and hand-made Oriental lamps give a mysterious Eastern feel; then, a classic European bookcase and a sharp corner revealing a flagrantly saucy, boudoir-style lounging area, change the concept radically.

The next step involves a leap of faith: there's a small balcony with two tables à deux — and below, a sexy, French restaurant decked out in burgundy and cream, complete with musician's stand and grand piano and huge double height glass windows exposing a vast paved garden beyond. It is a bit like Alice's journey down the rabbit hole — fantastical, disorientating, but ultimately rewarding.

One private room, booth seating, sofas for relaxing, a small lounge area in the middle of the restaurant, a bar and some outdoor tables and chairs beneath a white canopy were all designed by young furniture designer Andi Lim, while the overall concept was devised by D'Harcour. And what does he have to say about his creation? "As with the Nine Muses of Greek Mythology, we want to inspire, offer some moments of dreaming, and give elements of mystery and surprise." Check it out.

Left The entrance to the Nine Muses Club is mysterious, yet elegant. An Indonesian stupa on top of the door gives a signal, according to the owner, of "classic sophistication reminiscent of a European age conflicting with Asian values."

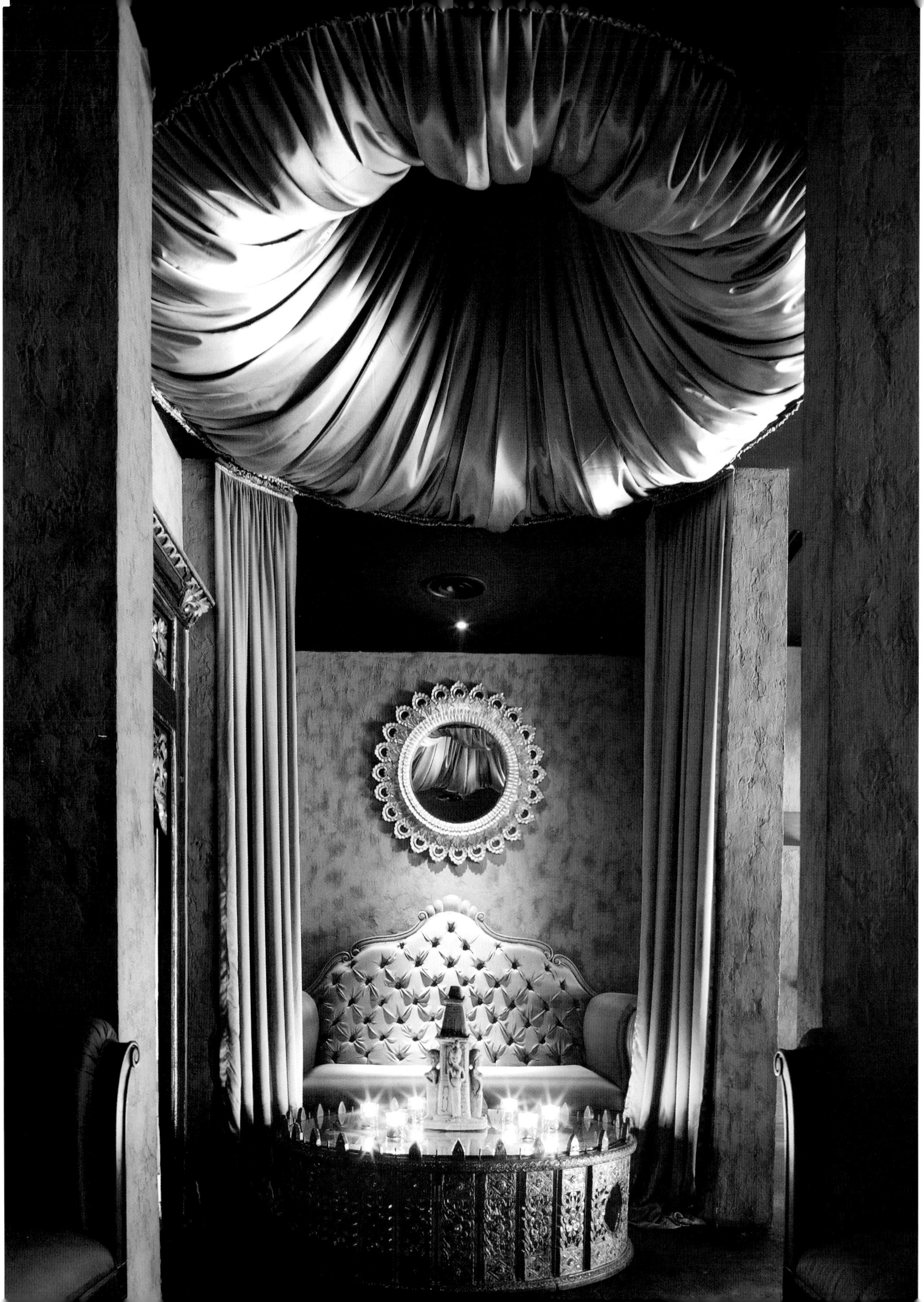

Left On the cusp of entering the restaurant proper is a luxe, silky day bed adorned by a Baroque mirror, giving an almost shocking, bordello-style allure.

Above A small private dining room on the upper level is furnished in classic French style. It affords lovely views over the garden below.

Above Young blood: Andi Lim, a talented young Indonesian designer educated in Australia, who has his own line of mostly residential furniture called JOOP, blends Asian and classic styles in the interiors. Using local materials, such as bamboo, he designed and manufactured all the furniture in the club. The upstairs balcony adjacent the "boudoir" is ideal for couples.

Left The interior is an eclectic mix of old and new that is somehow cohesive and coherent. Here an antique wedding chest from Palembang in Sumatra complete with Asian art, as well as old paintings and reproductions on slatted mauve silk walls, mix with elegant French-style chairs and sturdy tables.

Below At center of the club is a loungey area with low level seating clustered around a teak table. A condiment box from Northern Thailand sits atop it.

Opposite top Teasing the guest, the layout and interior concept of the Nine Muses Club awakens all the senses. The medieval-style candlelit cloister with Buddha head from Cambodia is reminiscent of an Asian temple, while the authentic leather bookcase at the far end is entirely European.

Opposite bottom An outdoor terrace covered by a flowing, white canopy seats 20 diners. It overlooks the large garden, paved with cement and inset stones, a stage for musicians and a number of large jackfruit, *jambu*, mango and longan trees. Lit up at night with sparkling fairy lights, the setting is romantic — and entirely unexpected.

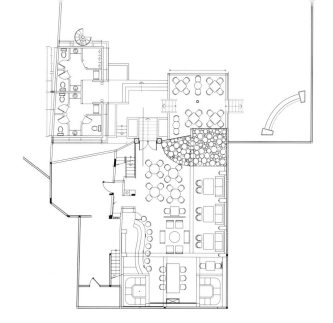

XLOUNGE, CHARCOAL, VERTIGO

When eight friends, many of whom had been at school together in San Francisco in the '90s, decided to get together and take Jakarta's night scene by storm, they were lucky to secure the top two floors of Plaza Semanggi. It proved to be the perfect location for the three-in-one venue they had in mind. It was spacious, it afforded great views over the city and to the domed auditorium below, and it was easily accessible.

"To just have one floor with one concept wouldn't have had any impact," explains co-owner Felix Denanta, "There are so many more things that can be done from a design point of view if you have a bigger area." To create that impact, the Gang of Eight enlisted the services of designers Antony Liu and Jeffrey Budiman — and asked them to steer clear of the usual dark, dull den style. They wanted a club, lounge and restaurant that showcased modern Jakarta in all its glory.

Even though the three venues are spread over two floors, they are all accessed from a common entrance and are unified by a huge reinforced glass wine tower at the core. This emerges from a sea of pebbles adjacent the entrance and rises vertically to cut through a void in the higher floor. According to Liu, with its up lighting and glinting glass and steel, it acts as the "central focal point" of the venue. Around are an exposed steel and translucent glass staircase, walkways made from reinforced glass with wood and pebbles below, and black granite and exposed concrete and plaster walls — all executed in a fairly rigid geometrical parti.

This rigidity was a key component in the design. "We wanted to create a space that is dedicated to the architectural way," explains Liu. All the bespoke details are "more architectural than interior in nature." Any "unnecessary feminine or sweet touches" were eschewed in favor of utilitarian materials (such as iron grilles and exposed concrete walls) and linear forms.

Right A flamed granite reception desk, exposed concrete walls and a uniformly grey palette greet guests. Alleviated partly by a huge iron grille and spots on the floor highlighting the textures of the stone, the overall effect is nevertheless austere. This is a serious venue for serious partying.

On the first floor, XLounge features custom-designed low-level furniture, sisal carpets and cool curtains, while Charcoal, a Japanese restaurant, sports a decorative installation filled with charcoal hanging atop the windows that run the perimeter of the restaurant. Simple low *merbau* tables with a central grill for teppanyaki are fuss free. A tatami-mat section with seating on the floor, and a couple of private rooms complete this simple eatery.

Above, in the apex of the building, is Vertigo. Here a central dance floor is surrounded by low-level seating as well as some custom-crafted roughly rendered *merbau* high tables with steel supports. Inset in these are small glowing blue LED lights. Further illumination is provided by two walls of steel rope-like lights that dangle beneath twisted metal stalks; taking their inspiration from the futuristic film *The Matrix*, their organic forms balance the rectangular rigidity of the club.

Opposite top Lounging zone extra-ordinaire: custom-crafted sofas and benches are divided from neighboring nooks by floaty curtains and geometric design. Since in opened in December 2004, the lounge has been the venue of choice to see and be seen.

Opposite below Swirling and geometric metalwork is used extensively in this site. Found on windows and used as space dividers, it adds to the industrial feel of the venue.

Above and right In the Japanese restaurant, Charcoal, there is a mix of low level seating (above) and private rooms and Western-style teppanyaki tables (on right). Orange vitrage lit from below gives a fiery effect in the private rooms, where floor-to-ceiling sliding doors can be shut for extra privacy.

Above The entire top floor is given over to Vertigo, where a large dance floor is surrounded by sectioned lounging areas on the perimeter and long high tables in roughly rendered *merbau* with attendant bar stools. Lighting is innovative, while circular iron grille works slide, allowing partitions to be removed or retained.

Opposite top An industrial effect is achieved with the use of steel and translucent glass in walkways and staircase, yet this is softened with natural pebbles and wood.

Opposite bottom The double height wine cooler is the central cohesive element in the club. Rising from the lower floor and breaking through into the club section of Vertigo, it is clad in glass and metal.

KUALA LUMPUR

FEAST VILLAGE

A type of up-market food court, with swanky outlets and swish decor, Feast Village sets new standards for the hospitality industry. Dubbed as KL's new gastronomic landmark, it certainly beats other similar hubs in the design stakes. Slightly chaotic and somewhat deconstructed, it is classy and quality-driven nonetheless.

Of course, the food court concept is as old as Asia itself. Typically a number of different stalls are set around a communal seating area — and patrons order dishes from a variety of vendors. Feast Village differs in that diners choose a particular restaurant in which to base themselves, but are then invited to order from as many of the venues as they wish. Situated in the basement of the revamped Starhill Gallery, more than a dozen outlets cluster round meandering pathways. All are connected, all semi open-plan with a mix 'n' match aesthetic, and, as none are fully enclosed, the atmosphere is buzzy, flexible and fluid.

Covering 4,300 sq m (46,300 sq ft) and seating over 1,000 diners, Feast Village is large by any standards. The overall design was masterminded by Yuhkichi Kawai of Design Spirits studio, but several of the restaurants have separate individual designers. Kawai-san was given a brief by YTL Properties, the operators of Starhill, to create a village that incorporated two elements — rustic and ethnic. He rose to the challenge by using materials from all over Asia — rice paper from Japan, granite from China, slate and ikat from Indonesia, silk from Thailand, wood from Burma, and more — and interpreted them in a modern way. As a result, Feast Village is a celebration of Asia, showcasing its design, its art, its multi-ethnicity and its food.

Take MyThai, for example. Owned and operated by Thailand's Jim Thompson Group, it was conceptualized by Warner Wong Design in Singapore to take the fabled hospitality of Jim Thompson, the man at his house on the *klong*, and bring it into a casual

Right Visually engaging, the Village Bar utilizes all sorts of bottles for columns and space dividers. Designer Yuhkichi Kawai said he got the inspiration for these from the supermarket! Different parts of the space are characterized by different seating: A row of Philippe Starck's Louis V Ghost Chairs contrast with animal printed upholstery on the bar stools.

Above left The stunning entrance to MyThai features a swirling noodle motif in steel, and floor-to-ceiling columns made from Thai celadon tea cups. Fresh and original, it sets the style within.

Right top A tall bottle "tower" stands at the entrance to Village Bar with Vansh behind. Both ethnic and rustic, but modern too, Feast Village is a celebration of Asian food — and Asian design and materials. Customers can cross-order from all 13 outlets, meaning you can have Malay food, Korean BBQ, dim sum and steak on one table. Just place your order at the restaurants and your food will be sent to the venue you are seated at.

Right below One of the seating options at MyThai are a series of Thai-style *salas*, draped in fabric and entirely suited for lounging. The *sala* is an open-sided pavilion traditionally found in rural Thailand, and nowadays often found in modern gardens where it has been reinvented as a gazebo.

restaurant setting. Thus, Thai motifs and food concepts from outdoor street cuisine are utilized in a modern version of "Jim's House" (see plan at right). MyThai has a double meaning: It is Jim Thompson's take on Thailand, but it also means "silk" in Thai — so Thai silk, concrete casts of breeze blocks used at the Thompson house, columns of celadon tea cups and seating booths in the form of intimate Thai *salas* are all used, along with *nyatoh* wood and a concrete floor.

Just across the walkway is Kawai-san's central Village Bar, where five varying angled counters give five different views of Feast Village. Thousands of recycled bottles in brown and green clear glass form large pillars and space dividers, while ethnic pendant lamps hang in profusion from above. If Indian is more your thing, head to Vansh next door: Run by the award-winning Rang Mahal in Singapore, it was also designed by Warner Wong as a mod-Bollywood joint. A wonderfully textural and exotic adobe interior wall inset with glittering glass is a reinterpretation of the Rajasthani tribal mud wall and, according to Wong Chiu Man of Warner Wong, the design is "at once spicy, tribal, contemporary, and very flexible in seating arrangements." Curry, anyone?

Above Boxy ceiling panels in *nyatoh* above the MyThai food counters house an extraction system, while in the open areas they conceal lights that cast a leafy light pattern on the whole dining area. This was intentionally manipulated to try to recreate the outdoor dining options at the Jim Thompson museum house in Bangkok.

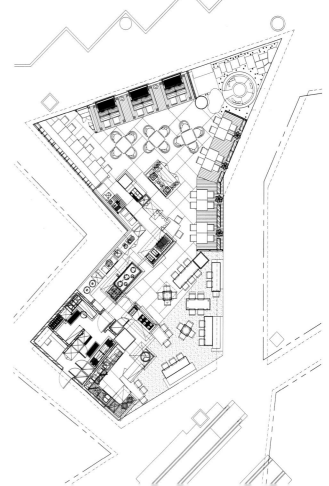

Opposite and below Hot stuff! Vansh's embellished interior includes a mock-tribal wall in mixed plaster, paint and bits of grass; rattan, raffia and colored glass pendant lights; and wood laminate tables with spicy, colorful fabrics casually arranged.

Opposite bottom Word perfect: A semi-transparent "wall" made from plywood and MDF in a variety of finishes features Hindi scrolls with writings from famous Indian poets. It sheathes the outer perimeter at Vansh, offering privacy on the one hand, but allowing interaction with other areas on the other.

Above Crazy paving: Maze-like paths, in a variety of materials and styles, connect the outlets. Made from stone, granite and timber, the texture varies every meter or so creating a somewhat uneven progression through the Feast Village. Kawai-san says that he sees Feast Village as a "fun place to stroll around" and "if you stop to eat and drink that is great too."

This page and opposite Flower power: Although not technically part of Feast Village, the floral-themed Tiffin Bay is also designed by Design Spirits and is situated on a higher floor in Starhill Gallery. Illuminated by a fiber optic curtain wall with a waterfall effect on one side and huge double height windows that drop down to the Starhill atrium below, it is an airy eerie perched seemingly in the sky. Serving pastries, chocolates, ice cream, tea and coffee during the day and transposing into a jazz and cocktail lounge by night, it is a vibrant space. Clusters of oversized sofas and plump chairs, upholstered in hippy-drippy flower prints, are artfully arranged around glass-topped tables. Tones are pastel and pretty; the vibe carefree and cool.

EEST

The Westin Kuala Lumpur is a charismatic, compact hotel situated in the business and shopping district along Jalan Bukit Bintang. The aesthetic here is upscale mod, with a clean-lined lobby, excellently designed F & B outlets and rooms with awe-inspiring views of the Petronas twin towers. The vibe is buzzy and business-like, the philosophy one of "renewal, both instinctive and personal."

But it isn't all about form. Function, too, is close to the hearts of the folks at the Westin — and they seek to offer a new level of genuine, non-prejudiced, yet unpretentious, service. This is encapsulated into both staff training, and the amenities on offer.

One of these is the pan-Asian restaurant, EEST. As the name and the different types of cuisine suggest, EEST straddles East and West in a thoroughly contemporary manner. There are five distinct styles of Asian food, the décor is a sublime mix of Asian materials and sleek Western forms, and the atmosphere is relaxed, yet dynamic. Its designer, Singapore-based Ed Poole, sums up: "In simplest terms, EEST is the manifestation of Asian craft articulated in Western neo-minimalism. It is part cosmopolitan chic, part ethnic style."

If this sounds a bit confusing, don't let the lingo put you off. Head up to the floor above the lobby, cross a small dark timber "bridge" where the lifts exit — and enter the lofty, light-filled space. You'll immediately feel uplifted, partly because the dark lift lobby temporarily deprives your senses so that visuals are heightened once you enter, and partly because the space itself is so stunning. Stretching over 827 sq m (8,900 sq ft) of floor space comprising private dining rooms, lounging areas, dining areas and open kitchens, it is loosely themed around a modernist interpretation of the traditional Asian courtyard.

After the space planning was completed, Poole sourced materials from all over Asia, then reinvented them in novel ways. Custom-made recycled aluminum tiles with an ancient *zhou* motif are used on ceilings, while flooring is in teak and hand-made tiles made from raw compressed volcanic ash from the Merapi volcano in central Java. Walls are in arabescato marble, glass and volcanic stone, and padded Thai silk panels add texture and softness.

At the entrance, which has a space-age Japanese diner feel, sexy padded chocolate brown leather day beds, the arms of which cleverly double up as back rests, are perfect for pre-dinner lounging. Else-where, "adz" finished teak tables and counters with a stainless steel edge trim, woven *abaca* chairs with Balinese water buffalo cushions and Thai silk back pillows, and shiny occasional tables made from natural *batong* pieces (a type of barnacle) are beautifully finished. The overall effect is intelligent, sensual and stylish — in keeping with the upbeat ethos of the hotel.

Right The lift lobby at the entrance to EEST is dark and dusky; the feeling inside lofty and light. A long bar greets guests: on right is the restaurant proper, on left the private dining rooms and lounge.

Left and below Counters are fashioned from volcanic stone and offer elevated dining space for bar aficionados. Woven *abaca* chairs were made by a company outside Kuala Lumpur that exclusively employs disabled men. *Abaca* is a natural material made from banana fiber and is also known as Manila hemp. Sections of the metallic ceiling are made from old coca cola cans from central Java, illustrating Poole Associates' commitment to recycling wherever possible.

Oposite top and bottom Named after Asian spices, private rooms all have fabulous views. Each is individually themed in different colors and layouts, while the Tamarind and Cinnamon rooms behind a gold wall seat 12 each — or may be joined to seat 24.

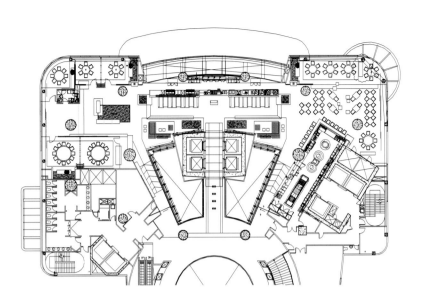

Above Waiting room: Sexy padded loungers, custom-made in Kuala Lumpur, have mounted lights underneath the larger bench seats for futuristic effect. Even though guests may dine here, it is often the place where they have a drink before going through to the restaurant proper.

Opposite top A cluster of private dining rooms opens onto a central "courtyard" with a stone pond filled with black river pebbles. Made from solid volcanic stone quarried in

Bali with a serrated finish to make the water "dance" as it travels down the wall, it is a cooling, calm space, ideal as a pre-function area or cocktail party space. Behind may be seen a floating water feature with cast aluminum vessel enclosed by an arabescato marble wall that ties in with the design of the lobby for a seamless transition.

Opposite bottom For the "adz" finished teak tables, the timber was scooped out with a chisel to create a textural effect.

THE DINING ROOM & BAR

Much of Asia's colonial architectural heritage has either been torn down or fallen down. Development on prime land is the reason for the former; the latter is a result of neglect, apathy or lack of funds. Malaysia, which houses a plethora of extant civic and residential edifices built during the colonial era, straddles the middle ground in this respect. Many such buildings are dilapidated at best, virtual ruins at worst.

Some, however, have been rescued, revitalized — and restored to their former grandeur. The old residence of the Federated Malay States' colonial administrators is a case in point. Comprising two properties known as the Carcosa Seri Negara in jungle parkland in central Kuala Lumpur, they were originally built from 1896 to 1904. Featuring expansive verandahs and high ceilings and built largely in wood, they were wonderfully suited to the tropical climate. However, after a century of wear and tear, both were riddled with termites and in a precarious state. A timely intervention has saved them.

Their complete renovation was overseen by GHM (General Hotels Management), a company justly known for its stylish, design-worthy hotels. Even though Carcosa Seri Negara is owned by the Government of Malaysia, GHM currently manages the hotel. With 13 sumptuous suites, function and banquet rooms, fine dining and service within a setting of manicured lawns and lake gardens, the hotel is both a fitting testament to the past as well as a celebration of the Malaysia of today.

If you can't afford to stay at the hotel, a meal at The Dining Room comes highly recommended. Situated in what was the official guesthouse known as the King's House, you sweep up the drive, alight beneath the porte cochère, ascend some steps to enter a galleried hall — and are ushered into the sumptuous restaurant. Classic is the adage here: you'll be served unadulterated fine French food with attentive formal service amidst surrounds that are luxurious, comfortable, impressive certainly, but never ostentatious.

Left A feast for the senses: A break in the massive dining room has been achieved by the addition of two false archways. Restored Prince of Wales prints and copies of the same adorn the bold-striped walls, while gold trimming on plates and decorative gold motifs on the chairs speak of high glamour.

The décor has all the trademarks of virtuoso interior designer Jaya Ibrahim. Known for masterminding the interiors at the Dharma-wangsa hotel in Jakarta, as well as numerous private residences, Ibrahim's style is supremely refined. Sensuous layering of fabrics, custom-crafted elaborately ornamental furniture, a dusky color palette and ample proportions contribute to a room that is the epitome of elegance. Deceptively simple at first glance, the room opens to reveal a vaulted central section, one private four-seater nook, as well as a colonial-style faux-verandah bar.

You'll easily find yourself succumbing to its charms. Silk-clad chandeliers illuminate candlesticks and canapés; gold-rimmed plates glitter beneath pleated shades on standing lamps; and soft melodies emanate from a glossy grand piano. The icing on the cake? The mesmeric, all-pervading scent of tuberoses.

Left On entering the Carcosa Seri Negara, guests are greeted by a large galleried hall, the ceiling of which resembles that of a European church. It is separated from the restaurant by this giant antique screen, which forms a buffer but allows guests to peek within.

Above Window dressing: Every item in the restaurant has been carefully chosen for a multi-layered sensory effect. Four-ply Jim Thompson silk curtains in gold tones are so thick they have the appearance of nearly standing up; they are accompanied by playful ribbons and rosettes in red. The chandeliers are originals: Sheathed in silk and topped by a cute turban, they stretch the length of the hall. Bold striped fabric from Germany covers walls, while the standing lamp shades are pleated for added texture.

Above The entire dining hall is carpeted with a red-and-gold toned Ibrahim-designed carpet; this switches to gold and beige in the upper part of the Carcosa. In the restaurant it highlights the gold decorative details — on cushions, dining plates and elaborate chair arms.

Above and opposite The adjacent bar, previously on a side verandah, has been enclosed for airconditioned comfort. Nonetheless, the furnishings and décor mimic the types of open-air spaces where terrace tipples would have been imbibed in the past. Wooden louvers cast shadow on the marble floor, and colonial-style chairs and tables with woven rattan tabletops echo those of an earlier era. An imposing dark wooden bar and various old maps and watercolors of Malay scenes add atmosphere — and élan.

GONBEI

Design Spirits, an interior design company that was set up in September 2003 by Yuhkichi Kawai, is the creative force behind the restaurant. YTL, Malaysia's high-profile property and hospitality firm, is the instigator. Starhill Gallery, a shopping center that underwent a total revamp by YTL in 2005 to reinvent itself as Kuala Lumpur's premier retail space, is the venue. Gonbei is the name.

Gonbei translates as a "typical farmer" in ancient Japan. Such people had a deep-seated tradition of heartfelt hospitality, and the restaurant seeks to emulate this tradition. Entrance is via a bamboo arched tunnel representing the structure of a traditional farmhouse — and just inside are three iron pots cooking rice over a fire. From here it is a hop, skip and a jump into the multi-space restaurant, where five sections, each with a separate counter, offer teppanyaki, sushi, robatayaki, tempura and sake. The whole is a feast for the eye, as well as for the palette.

"At Design Spirits we aim for a spirit of craftsmanship and an earnest attitude," explains Kawai-san. "An essence makes a space. We search for that essence in order to create a space with long life. As craftsmen, these are our design spirits."

He goes on to explain that the concept for the 558-sq-m (6,000-sq-ft) Gonbei was to house "five separate (isolated) counters in one restaurant" and self-deprecatingly describes the décor as "just a surface; just make-up on the face, nothing related to the heart."

Nevertheless, the interiors display a marked originality, be they heartfelt or not. Stacked bottle and blue-and-white ceramic bowl partitions help delineate space, while light-toned *changal* floors and counters imbue the entire space with a soft pleasing glow. Whimsical references to place are thoughtfully — and effectively — executed: A semi-private sunken seating area is backed by a wall of assorted *tenugui*, cotton hand towels that were popular 300 years ago in Japan as *kabuki* actors used them as name cards. Elsewhere, a wall, covered in colorful *chi-yo-ga-mi* or lithographs, reveals itself as a sliding door or *fusuma*. When this is opened, it shows another wall covered in *kamon* or traditional Japanese family crests. "If a VIP comes to the restaurant two days in a row, or a party or a function is taking place, you can create a different ambience within two minutes," explains Kawai-san.

This multi-functionality is only one aspect of the restaurant. Others include the variety of cuisine and the quality of the sake. And the restrooms shouldn't be excluded: Kabuki masks depict gender outside, and bamboo replaces the faucet inside.

Right A semi-private space achieved by an innovative Japanese ceramic pottery "wall" cocoons diners from other areas in Gonbei. The back wall is covered with Japanese handkerchiefs, offering respite from the pale wood finishing elsewhere.

Opposite Different local hardwoods are used throughout Gonbei to further the trad farmhouse theme. The floor is covered in *changal* as are the counter tops, while grained *maranti* is used on walls. Japanese blue-and-white fabric is used for cushion covers on the robust chairs.

Below Displaying a marked originality, the restaurant is divided and clad by semi-permanent partitions. Here stacked wine bottles are used as partitions and sake barrels are used as cladding. The rustic counter and chunky chairs are earmarked for those who wish to dine alone or in peace and quiet.

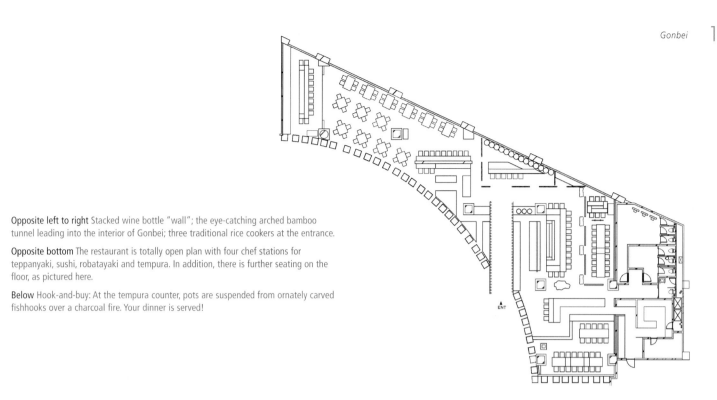

Opposite left to right Stacked wine bottle "wall"; the eye-catching arched bamboo tunnel leading into the interior of Gonbei; three traditional rice cookers at the entrance.

Opposite bottom The restaurant is totally open plan with four chef stations for teppanyaki, sushi, robatayaki and tempura. In addition, there is further seating on the floor, as pictured here.

Below Hook-and-buy: At the tempura counter, pots are suspended from ornately carved fishhooks over a charcoal fire. Your dinner is served!

SEVENATENINE

Designed by the ebullient Ed Poole and owner/operated by a team of seven like-minded individuals, sevenatenine opened in February 2006. It has all the creative credentials: There is celeb chef Emmanuel Stroobant in the kitchen; the environment is indoor-outdoor with fab views of the Petronas Towers; there are cool tunes and an even cooler ice resin bar; and there is space for all kinds of diners — at communal tables, on lush sofa-beds next to a reflecting pond, at dining tables or high up at the bar.

And about time too, you might say. KL is known on the club circuit and there are plenty of mid-level restaurants, but it has been pretty low on the sophisticated, yet informal, multi-space restaurant/bar in the past. All that has changed now, as sevenatenine more than adequately fills the gap.

Advocating a relaxed dining experience amidst the brouhaha of the metropolis, sevenatenine has both urban and rustic elements beneath a smooth, contemporary veneer. There is a luxurious function room on the mezzanine, while the alfresco curved bridge facing Petronas Towers is altogether more recreational. This area is climate controlled with ceiling fans, aircon and a glass perimeter wall that protects the property from outside traffic noise and pollution. Clean, modern lines are softened by the semi-circular floor plan, and elements like stainless steel fans and ultra-mod Accupunto chairs are countered by a driftwood paneled ceiling and timber Trident tables in a driftwood finish. A mainly organic palette of colors and a lot of natural light are wonderfully enervating.

Tropical cocktails, a DJ spinning the latest Euro-Asian chill-out grooves and a kitchen that caters to the discerning palette are only part of the offering. sevenatenine has an eco-friendly ethos too. Designers, Poole Associates, are always looking at ways to eliminate waste by recycling or using everyday materials found to hand. If they do use new timbers, they replant ten times the number of trees they use. Here, old railway sleepers have found new life as flooring and the space is a good example of the company's policy of trying to use less air conditioning. "Only one third of the space is fully climate cooled by mechanical means," explains Poole, "the rest uses passive solutions to bring down the air temperature."

Housed in the super elegant Ascott building, sevenatenine was designed to emulate a resort in the city. Welcoming "wallflowers, kooks and the conventional", the folks at sevenatenine declare that you won't want to leave! "However, we want you to go," they say, "so that you can come back."

Left Tall LED panels with sheet covers that can be programmed to any of 16 million colors contribute greatly to the mood at any given time at sevenatenine. They are also visible from the street, so tend to attract new clientele.

Opposite The entire facade of the building was removed to accommodate an extended deck at ground level and an enlarged mezzanine floor. Existing columns support this new mezzanine which now pushes out directly from the building's frontage.

Above The mezzanine level is used for more formal dining (there is also a fully air conditioned dining rom here, too), while the ground floor is more casual. Timber floors are made up from 400-year-old railway sleepers sourced from Borneo. Apparently, when the floor was laid, there was still a faint scent of the railway, evoking the romantic notion of hundreds of thousands of leisurely hours spent traveling over this floor via train carriage.

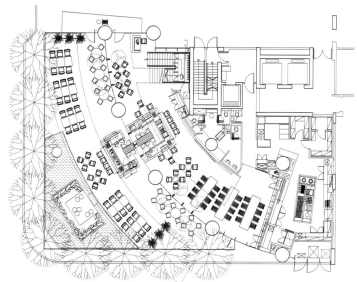

Above Alfresco dining can be combined with lounging on the open-air, glass covered terrace with views of the Petronas Towers. Fully surrounding the property is a 2.45 m (8 ft) high wall of glass that serves to keep cool air in and prevent noise from escaping. Chairs and sofas are covered with Lino Bianco slipcovers — and LED lighting makes them almost glow at night.

Right top Timber tables are chairs were treated with a lime wash to introduce a slightly sun-bleached effect suitable for an outdoor venue.

Right bottom Bar stool sourced from the Accupunto range. A father and son collaboration, Accupunto designs chairs with a unique pin system that is based on the ancient practice of acupressure. When the weight shifts on the chair, the pins shift on their axis and support the user following his or her contour. Moreover, they combine their function with a snazzy form.

Opposite A large white sculptural panel on the stairs is interesting for textural appeal.

SINGAPORE

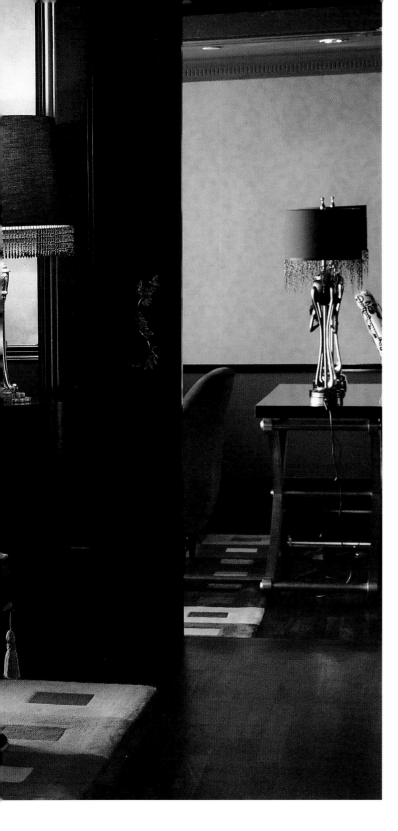

BOLD

The partnership between Asian hoteliers Grace International and Australian interior design company Indez proved fruitful when the boho-chic Scarlet Hotel flung open its glass doors with red lacquered handles at the end of 2004. Many declared it a marriage made in heaven. Situated within a row of heritage buildings in Chinatown, the hotel interiors signified a departure for supposedly staid Singapore: boudoir-bold, with a red-and-gold palette and lashings of luxe, its design was lauded and applauded by local and international press alike.

It's not surprising, therefore, that its bar has become the hang-out of choice for local fashionistas and the advertising crowd as well as hotel guests. Aptly named Bold, it is a snug cutie hideaway for those in the know. From its black leather padded bar to its custom-designed furniture and fittings, it oozes audacity. "As the name implies," explains Michael Tan, Grace International's Creative Director, "this bar is for uninhibited encounters."

Situated adjacent the lobby, Bold has a seductive, clubby feel — with more than a dash of sex appeal. Ideal for the romantic rendezvous, it sports a variety of seating clusters and a curvaceous, marble-topped bar. There is also a private "meeting room" leading off it: Called the Sanctum, it barely accommodates a table with a granite top and customized black lacquer chairs, and is intended for corporate groups. It seems unlikely, however, that much business would get done here.

For Bold, it has to be said, is far more pleasure dome than official home. Its over-the-top decor is dramatic and intimate in turns, with daring colors, forms and details. Chairs, playing with scale with oversized backrests and arms, are used to counter low ceilings and there are lots of reflective surfaces to create sparkle and a sense of "being seen." Cushions of silk and chenille with beads, sashes and swags vie with deliciously decadent upholstered chaise-longues.

Left On the fringe: Gold-fringed black leather poufs and over-sized, high-backed chairs at the entrance are once seen, never forgotten. All the furniture in the hotel was conceptualized by Grace International and customized by design firm Indez using local manufacturers.

On the floor Indonesian walnut shines, whilst above a striking gold mesh ceiling is backed with grey mirror panels. In one section a brash, blocky rug forms a geometric element to the space: this and the grid ceiling act as a counterpoint to the free forms of the bar, window screens, rounded furniture and the oval Sanctum.

Singapore may have been a little slow off the mark to respond to the global demand for the bijou boutique hotel, but in Asia it is a leader in this genre. Admittedly the Scarlet wasn't the first in the category to open, but Bold is definitely the premier — and so far only — hotel bar that displays such a level of creativity. For the ultimate end to an evening out, have a nightcap there — and check into one of the hotel's saucy suites afterwards.

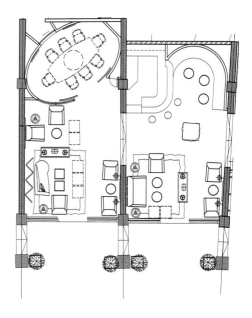

Above Club soda? The free-form black leather padded bar with under-counter lighting and black-and-white marble top has a clubby appeal. Ringed by black suede banquette seating edged with white by Dedar Fabrics, it is just the ticket for a postprandial tipple.

Opposite Custom-made classic lamps with funky shades in a variety of finishes, sizes and designs give a bordello feel, as do the gold-and-red signature colors enhanced with moody, luminous fabrics from Dutch interior fabric specialists Russell & Harvey.

THE BUTTER FACTORY

Creating an environment that combines popular culture with music, graphic design, a quirky aesthetic and a space to get "seriously slouchy" in, the Butter Factory is unique in Singapore's nightlife scene. Here, the philosophy is part and parcel of the décor; and the décor is reflective of the owners' aim to be an "urban-driven venue" that blends hip hop, rhythm & blues and street art.

The entrance sets the tone: Its circumference is one huge flaming red-lipped mouth, à la the Stones logo (tonsils and tongue to be added later). It is attention grabbing, populist, sexy and smoochy, and — like all good things — gives a taste of what is to come. This comes in the form of an extravagantly conceived two-room club, with Room One dedicated to art and Room Two a tongue-in-cheek design depiction of a home.

Room One or the Art Bar (see right) is dominated by over 150 graphic renderings of characters hanging from the ceilings and walls. These are set against a roughly rendered backdrop, with exposed concrete bar, low-slung armchairs upholstered in white with an industrial fluorescent stripe in candy pink, and floor-to-ceiling glass windows with black drapes. The emphasis is on the global graphic art talent, and a multimedia projector screens lives of the artists, character-related animation films and anything else that takes the owners' fancy. This is the chill-out zone — it's artsy, there's a Hoxton vibe, it's a work in progress.

The far larger Room Two, the hub of the club, comprises a kooky representation of a home. An aluminum-coated bar is rendered to represent a kitchen, with kitschy oven and fridge doors and an extraction hood; there's a funky outdoor area with barbecue grills from an outdoor supplier and Philippe Starck stools like upside down flower pots in primary colors. "This is the picnic area," explains Bobby Luo, co-owner and creative director. For those who want more comfort, there is the "living room" area, a comfy lounge, or the "deck" with umbrellas, fake trees and loungers, as well as a VIP lounge in the form of a bedroom in luxe red.

All these are arranged round the crème-de-la-crème of the room: a dance floor with a special epoxy based coating with a controlled sheen that looks like a swimming pool! Cool lighting makes it glow at night, while plastic grate edging, diving board, public-pool style blue mosaic tiling and metal accessories like an outdoor shower and pool stairs, ensure Luo and his team get full marks for creative credentials. "We want people to feel at home here," says Luo, only slightly ironically.

Right Going global: Graphic characters suspended from the ceiling in the Art Bar at the Butter Factory are by a bevy of global artists — from countries as diverse as Israel, Croatia, Switzerland and more. Many are by Australian artist JeremyVille — an artist, toy designer and clothing producer from Sydney.

Above Bobby Luo worked closely with architect Song-por Tan of Axis.Point Design to conceive a space that is at once compact yet spacious. The duo wasn't afraid to mix the utilitarian with the luxurious or the kitschy with the cool, and they borrowed freely from street culture. The comic-book style works, from local and international graphic designers and web-page designers, anchor the club in a populist milieu.

Opposite Trip the light fantastic: Emphasizing how important lighting is in a club setting, no expense was spared on the lighting for bar counters and graphic walls at the Butter Factory. Cold Cathode Fluorescent lights (CCFL), a new technology that provides low ambient lighting, were used in these areas.

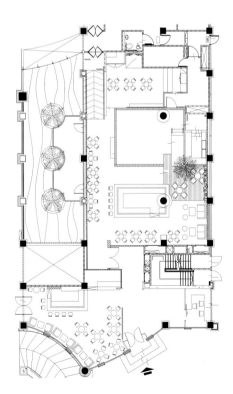

Opposite top left Small aqua-colored mosaic tiling, reminiscent of public pool changing rooms, forms the surrounds of the DJ console. Behind is a wall display of monochromatic graphics designed by :phunk studios. A four-partner graphic design firm in Singapore, it is also responsible for the lips at the entrance.

Opposite top middle The VIP lounge sports an over-the-top chandelier, walls plastered in scarlet shoe leather sheathed in sequins, and custom-crafted boxy glam glass side tables with lava lamps within. There's even a wardrobe front.

Opposite top right and below A semi-abstract and suggestive swimming pool feel around the dance floor is achieved with tongue-in-cheek detailing such as the diving board high counter clad in blue mosaic tiles and stainless steel grip bar with life-saving buoy, as well as the circumference pool "grating."

Opposite bottom Kitschy kitchen accoutrements line the stainless steel bar.

Right Home-gnome culture: The tongue-in-cheek outdoor BBQ area features garden gnomes, mini grills and wallpaper that simulates the great outdoors.

THE LINE

A collaboration between the Shangri-La hotel group and hospitality design guru Adam D Tihany, The Line is a bold buffet-style restaurant, bar and foodie shop located on the lower lobby level at Shangri-La Singapore. Strikingly contemporary, with a primary color scheme of orange, it is bright, bustling and big. It sprawls over an area of 1,350 sq meters (1,615 sq yards); it seats 410 people, with 113 seats available al fresco; and there are 16 food stations with a mouth-watering array of global ingredients and kitchen styles on display.

Unusually for a group that stresses its Asian roots and heritage, The Line is unabashedly Western in design and execution. Nevertheless its concept of busy communal dining, especially with the popularity of the buffet, is Asian in origin. This, plus the fact that it offers great value for money, has led to its rapturous reception in the hearts — and stomachs — of many a Singaporean.

The brief the Shang (as the hotel is affectionately known to locals) gave the Tihany design studio was for "a world-class restaurant with a modern, contemporary design that would compete with the latest high-end restaurants in Singapore and the world." Furthermore, they wanted the restaurant to work well during both day and night and to appeal to travelers and locals alike. In addition, it needed to showcase a variety of cuisines, as well as the freshness and excellence of the food.

The Line delivers on all the above, and what it may lack in romance and atmosphere, it more than makes up for in attitude. Its key design element is a vertical series of "orange-line" light boxes made from glass with fluorescent lighting that traverse the length of the space; these represent the line of progression that every ingredient goes through, from the fridge, to the cooking, to the buffet, to the diner. This, along with four custom-made films about the origins of food screened simultaneously on plasma panels, is gloriously high-tech.

Left Reading between the lines: Sixteen food stations, all slightly different, are located in The Line. At the display counter on right, long hanging lamps are made from polished chrome; they add extra illumination on kitchen activity.

The "line" theme is furthered in the geometric floor plan competently laid out for functionality, the boxy serving stations, a series of blue glass panels lit with halogen lights, white and grey lined zebrano marble floors, and a long backlit bar and shared high table. Equally sleek are the tables and chairs, Corian counters and open-plan kitchens (think shiny, aluminum and modern): All were custom-designed by the Tihany design studio and manufactured by local firms.

On any given day there are 70 chefs in the kitchens, countless wait staff with POS hand terminals and 2,000 plus diners, so The Line needs to run like a well-oiled machine. As Adam D Tihany is probably the most pre-eminent restaurant designer in the world, he would have known each and every detail that needed to be considered. The result, costing a neat S$7 million, was "exactly as he had envisaged!"

Below The futuristic long bar is underlit in the same way the light boxes are above. With high bar stools, it counteracts the high table that is offset at a right angle.

Above left High tea: A communal high table with bar-style seating is situated near the entrance.

Above middle On the perimeter of the restaurant bordering the garden is a glass-roofed greenhouse type area. All-white furniture is placed on a custom-designed carpet with an oval field pattern that provides relief from the linear stone patterning and general geometric forms found elsewhere. Adjacent is the al fresco dining section.

Above right Each food counter offers a different type of cuisine.

Right Down the line: The entrance to the restaurant is via a clean-lined staircase with steel balustrades.

the line

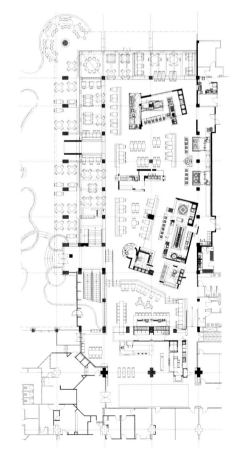

Top Plasmas, placed on various walls throughout, simultaneously screen custom-made art films on food: Designed by Adam D Tihany's son, they are named, Fish, Grain, Vegetables and Wine.

Above Silver PVC covered couches and utilitarian furniture are purposefully low-key and functional: at The Line the emphasis is always on the food.

Opposite Stacks of china plates — Tihany's design for Schönwald — line each kitchen counter. Staff uniforms were designed by local fashion designer Allan Ross.

CHINA ONE

Situated on the top floor of nine units in one of the godown blocks of Clarke Quay, China One is representative of a type of East/West interior design that is increasingly popular in Europe and the United States. Combining a Western aesthetic (in this case, think New York semi-industrial loft) with Asian furniture, furnishings and art (Shanghai style), it is a convincing example of successful Oriental/Occidental cross-fertilization.

Designer Ed Poole, who was constricted by a very tight budget, was inspired to combine new concrete with old wood because of an experiment he tried in his own home. "About 12 years ago, I bought the facade and part of the interior of an old apothecary shop on China Street in Singapore's Chinatown," he says, "and when I started renovating my flat, I wanted a neutral space of raw cement. Using the doors as paneling, I found I liked the combination of the brown timbers and mottled off-form concrete." Following the theme through into a commercial project was his next challenge.

Comprising a central bar (China One) sandwiched between two pool halls (Baize), the 697-sq-m (7,500-sq-ft) space measures only 65 m (213 ft) in width. When the client acquired it, it was divided into several different tenancies, all with different floor heights, ceiling and wall finishes and interior design. Poole knocked all the walls through, removed tons of brick and reinforced concrete as well as a giant aircon plant that was larger than a truck and opened up the ceilings to expose the rafters and roofs. The end result was the creation of a clear path down the entire nine units like "one long runway." "This central spine was the organizing factor that would dictate the three "rooms", the table arrangements, and so on," explains Poole.

China One is divided into loosely arranged separate spaces, one entirely filled with old silk-draped opium beds and reconditioned screens, another with low level 1950s Shanghai repro boxy leather armchairs, another with seating clustered around a plasma screen. Unifying the whole is a long wooden bar, custom crafted in Shanghai, with an asymmetric form that encourages conversation niches. Made from local timbers, it has an old cracked look "to give the top character." Many of the other pieces of furniture (bar stools, tables and so on) are reproductions made in the same factory, but some, such as the opium beds and medicine chests, are very old reconditioned pieces; others are totally new creations. Where they are unified is in the tobacco brown staining; this matches the leather seating and creates a minimalist feel while retaining the textures of Old Shanghai.

The two pool saloons situated on left and right are less dusky and atmospheric, more bright and light for obvious reasons. Nonetheless, they take their cue (pun intended) from China One's design: with well maintained billiard tables, ample seating, plasma screens and a Chinois-chic vibe, they are glassed off as they are smoke-free zones.

Left Reproduction 1950s boxy leather furniture from Shanghai beneath a painting of a Buddha head from one of the owners' private collection.

Above Old Shanghai is epitomized by such items of furniture as these opium beds. They are extremely old, and have been reconditioned beautifully.

Left Baize is the name given to the two pool saloons. Even though they lack the dusky atmosphere of China One, they maintain a link with the bar with the placement of Chinese lacquer furnitue. These two wedding cabinets with large metal fastenings are a case in point.

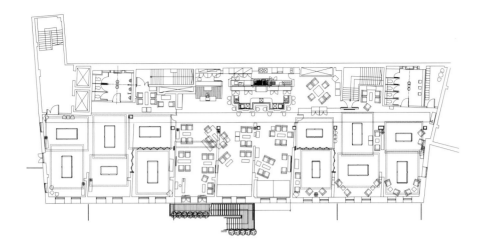

Opposite bottom All the furniture (including the long bar seen at back of photograph) was sourced from warehouses in Shanghai and/or reproduced at a factory there. "We tried to select compatible pieces that would work together," says Poole. "It was a real challenge to map out each piece and place it on the plan to fill the nine units adequately. A digital camera was a tremendous help in this process as there are about 240 items." Be it a rosewood table, an old ottoman, or an ancient opium bed — the pieces fit together like a puzzle.

Below Most of the wall-mounted screens are authentic doors from old homes or *hutongs* in Shanghai. However, the panels used to create the private pool rooms are hand-carved reproductions as they needed to be the exact right dimension for 36 panels. Bare bulbs in bird cages (seen here) and concealed spots cast light (and shadows) in interesting patterns on the textured walls.

THE CLIFF

Even though the folks at the Sentosa Resort & Spa are keen to downplay the undisputed drama of its evening-only restaurant, it has to be said that this is a place for occasion dining. Meticulously crafted by Yasuhiro Koichi of Spin Design using a powerful combo of glass, light, stone and water, The Cliff is very impressive. But, because of its al-fresco, poolside location, it doesn't have the intimidating touches of an over-formal restaurant.

There is no hushed atmosphere, starchy tablecloths, solid silver-ware or stolid service here. Rather, it is casual, outdoorsy, loungy and breezy — but sensuous, serene and sculptural too. Trees push up through wooden decking and ships' lights glimmer out over the ocean. The restaurant literally pulses with columns of illuminated blue glass, flickering candlelight, textured walls flowing with water, bamboo and brick, granite and grass. Yet, because there is space between the individual settings, and different types of tables and dining options, there is a relaxed informality to the whole.

Aptly serving fresh food inspired by the sea, The Cliff is dominated by a state-of-the-art central show kitchen. Glassed in, but open to the eyes of all, it makes for fascinating viewing. Dinner is dished up at a number of different seating options: there is the grey granite long bar offering 180-degree views over the sea, square tables for intimate dining, and benches with soft leather lounge chairs; excellent views seaward can also be had from tables on a lower platform, and a couple of communal dining tables are perfect for lone diners or larger gatherings. A semi-private pavilion "room," accessed by a granite bridge and suspended over water, has a beautiful round table, whilst another glassed-in area fronts the kitchen and a "wall" composed of tanks of seafood.

Yasuhiro, as with many other Japanese designers, is a wizard with texture and layering. A series of round aqua-blue glass sculptures,

Right Facing seaward, The Cliff's bar offers magnificent views over the ocean at night. Chick blinds may be lowered on rainy evenings.

Above The restaurant as seen from across the swimming pool by night. When the management decided it wanted a new signature restaurant, Spin felt it was important that its design should co-exist with the older hotel that was designed by Kerry Hill more than a decade ago. "We designed The Cliff bearing in mind the importance of a subtle balance between contrast and fusion with the existing hotel," explains Yasuhiro Koichi of Spin Design. Certainly, it stands, out, but never does it overwhelm within its existing poolside location.

Right Huge candles and LED lights illuminate the Seiki Torige aqua-blue stacked glass columns (at left of photograph) at the entrance. Here an over-water path gives access to the theatrical evening-only restaurant. On right is a "waterfall wall."

Opposite One of three aqua-toned glass round sculptures floats on a "pond" at the front of The Cliff. In the background the open-plan kitchen may be seen.

complete with underwater lighting and gurgling water, along with columns in the same glass, add more than a touch of theatricality to a splashy entrance. Designed by Spin, but realized by Japanese glass artist Seiki Torige, they surround over-water paths made from black granite with a pointed hammered finish at the front. Alongside is a water-wall artwork, over which water flows in a dizzying fashion. According to the designer who refuses to divulge how it is made: "It looks like a waterfall with the water being stopped but I am afraid I cannot tell you how this effect has been achieved — it's a trade secret!"

What is not a secret is that The Cliff is inspired by "tropical greens, the sea and the beautiful views from the restaurant." It is breathtakingly beautiful by night, it is fluid and elemental — and its naturalistic Asian garden ambience is both refreshing and peaceful. And once within the airy confines of the open-plan space, wherever you sit, there is plenty to look at.

Above The lower level of the restaurant with seaward views to the left.

Opposite top A floating pavilion "room" is beautifully illuminated by a sculptural gothic-style chandelier hanging above a centrally placed round table. All the lights were designed by Spin, as were the staff uniforms.

Opposite bottom All the furniture was custom-crafted by Spin using dyed teakwood. Different shapes for tables, and different flooring — wooden decking, beige terrazzo, green ceramic tiles — create different spaces within the open-plan restaurant. Tableware is carefully chosen and mainly sourced in Singapore.

CRYSTAL JADE GOLDEN PALACE

Red is the color of populist China. In the past, yellow was reserved for Emperors, gold likewise, but red was of the people. It sprang to prominence with the advent of communism, most notably with the evolution of the song *The East is Red*. This started out as a peasant love song, then became an Anti-Japanese anthem in World War II, and finally became a homage extolling Chairman Mao. Along with Mao's Little Red Book and the Red Star of China, its symbolism was assured.

Despite today's political and economic reforms, red still remains the color of China. Red (often accompanied by black) is popular in Chinese graphic design and Chinese furniture often was, and still is, lacquered red or black and then painted. The Chinese flag is red, and the red silk cheongsam is once again a popular item of clothing in China and elsewhere.

It is fitting, therefore, that local company Crystal Jade's high-end Chinese restaurant in the up-market Paragon building on Orchard Road uses a contemporary interpretation of Chinese red. Black wood, inspired by Chinese black ink, and vertical red-lacquered panels incorporating lights and glass for a futuristic shiny effect, are used for drama and spectacle at both the entrance and in the main dining hall. In fact, the designers at Spin Design studio took the red process one step further. "Actually, with this shiny red we tried to express water like a piece of modern art — a Water Garden with lights of lacquered shininess," they say.

This modernist treatment of the color red, and on a wider scale the use of the modern along with the traditional, is a recurring theme at Golden Palace. Some of the private rooms seek to offer a 21st-century interpretation of China, with very sleek leather panelling, over-sized graphic floral paintings and contemporary furniture and furnishings. Others combine a more trad sensibility with *donsu* panelled walls (*donsu* came to Japan originally under Chinese influence and are used to frame hanging scrolls in temples

Left The walls in the main Dining Hall set the scene for fine Teochew cuisine: Vertical red stripes on one intentionally represent Modern China, while tiles, historically used as a base for roofs in China, stacked one on top of the other are more traditional. Double-layered brass mesh standing lamps work well with antique finished ash wall and ceiling panelling, while furniture is a mix of old and new.

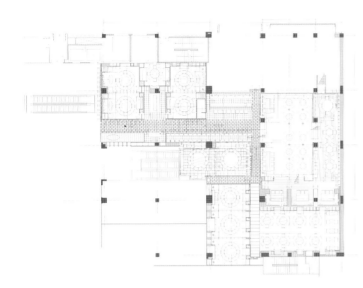

and shrines in Japan), classic high-backed Chinese chairs and round tables with lazy susans, as well as calligraphy artworks.

Elsewhere, new and old are mixed together for varying effects: in the Restaurant Hall a fusion of West and East is expressed in an extraordinary plaster-cast ceiling utilizing classic European motifs and a mirrored wall giving the illusion of the ceiling continuing forever. In the main Dining Hall, the feeling is sleek and chic, with a granite-topped bar, specially designed classic-with-a-twist furniture, brass mesh standing lamps and — of course — the Modern Chinese vertical panel wall in luminous red.

Golden Palace is large by any standards, but because it is subdivided into various sections and private rooms it never seems over-powering. Rather it exhibits a design unity with other Crystal Jade venues: Taking elements of old China's *yin* to counteract modern China's *yang* is not easy — and Spin Design has accomplished this balancing act with finesse.

Above One of the more severe private rooms that utilizes traditional themes for a Classic China feel. Sturdy, old-fashioned Chinese furniture and calligraphy artworks by Beijing artist Yan Yan (not seen) reinforce the Spin design brief.

Right A suitably dramatic black-and-red color palette characterizes the decor at Golden Palace.

Left A severe bar in black granite with lacquered cabinets behind is a central focal point at Golden Palace. In front is an illuminated glass sculpture by Seiki Torige welcoming guests. Spin describes the piece as like a "big flower vase," the surfaces of which have been treated to present a contemporary interpretation of an outdoor scene.

PS CAFÉ

Those in the know in Singapore have long patronized the café attached to the Project Shop store in Paragon shopping centre. With its yummy "international comfort food," rows of fashion and design magazines, friendly service and laid-back atmosphere, it has a loyal following of foodies and fashionistas alike. However, there's always been a downside. However good the music, however cute the waiter and however fresh the food — you can't escape the fact that you are munching in a mall. A mega-mall at that.

So, what great news to find the owners have expanded — and opened a new outlet. Eschewing the urban jungle, for well ... the jungle, PS Café is housed in a steel-and-glass Modernist building in the middle of tropical parkland. The place is Dempsey Road, the site of an old army barracks that is at once central, yet arboreal. Surrounded by tall trees, grassland and equatorial greenery, it is a location in a million.

The building was designed by partners Philip Chin, Peter Teo and Richard Chamberlain with the help of architect friend Aamer Taher of Aamer Taher Design Studios. Even though they are fashion designers, the trio has always taken care of the interiors of their stores and the original café, so fancied turning their hands to architecture for this one. Favoring an industrial aesthetic, they are keen on utilitarian materials and functionality: aircon ducts are exposed in their stores, and galvanized steel, rugged brick and wire mesh are used liberally.

The premise at PS Café was that every table in the "glass-box" structure should have a view. A previous old army canteen was totally demolished, and in its place a cool white-and-bright raw brick, steel and glass building with a white painted corrugated iron roof was erected. Much of the design was cost-driven, so the structure is fairly simple, yet functional. Divided into three loosely-connected spaces — a comfy lounging area, a boxy bar and a larger dining room — all look out through a front "wall" entirely sheathed in glass. Outside is an ample deck with a perimeter

Right The structure of PS Café itself is simple: a double iron roof allows for hidden wiring and also minimizes the noise of heavy rainfall, while the walls are made from steel and glass or white painted brick. All diners are angled towards the surrounding parkland for jungle views: in fact, the green from outside almost seems to permeate into the café itself.

wooden bench — and stunning views into a blanket of green. You couldn't be further from Singapore's downtown atmosphere, yet you're only a hop, skip and a jump from downtown.

This fledgling shares many similarities with its elder sibling. As with the Paragon café, interiors are trendy and unfussy. Mismatched wooden boards on the floor, a neutral color palette, retro custom-made '50s and '60s chairs and sofas upholstered in what Chin calls "old airport upholstery," a variety of blackboards for daily specials, and a magazine rack are all PS staples — as are some of the signature dishes. However, the space is much larger and there is minimal intervention within the setting. PS Café is truly a garden restaurant: If you want green food — fresh herbs and salads — in a green setting, this is a sure winner.

Opposite A rickety wooden pathway sets the tone for the arboreal eating experience ahead.

Left The central bar is made from rugged brick, with a stainless steel and wood top. A slightly lower ceiling is angled above it, to bring a different contour to the space and also to conceal the aircon vents. Magazines hang from hooks below the counter.

Top The Dining Room is refreshingly furnished with some custom-crafted pieces and some collected over the years. The kitchen (seen in background) is semi-concealed from diners with the use of shelving and ribbed glass at eye level, and functional cupboards below. However, movement and cooking can be seen/unseen from the dining room.

Above Chin and Teo are avid collectors of retro furniture, so when they needed to fill the café, they approached Malaysian company Fiske to custom make chairs, sofas and tables to their design. All the fabric — herringbone, stripes and squares — was sourced from the long-forgotten stock at the back of a Chinese fabric shop in Kuala Lumpur — little did the owner know he was sitting on a '70s goldmine!

MY HUMBLE HOUSE

Owned and operated by Singapore supremos Tung Lok Group, My Humble House is a dramatic formal restaurant for occasion dining. Offering modern interpretations of classic Chinese cuisine in spectacular surrounds, Asia's best is displayed here in high style.

"The idea was that the restaurant should be anything but humble," explains Tung Lok's founder and CEO Andrew Tjioe. Tjioe, who won the Asia Lifetime Achievement award in recognition of his contribution to the local F & B industry at Singapore's 2005 World Gourmet Summit, is a passionate proponent of excellence in all aspects of his business. From the food to the interiors to the service, Tjioe wanted only the best. Working with a visionary team — artist-musician Zhang Jin Jie of Beijing's Green T House, interior architect Antonio Eraso and lighting guru Kuro Mende — he turned his ideas into reality.

It started with the food: Since 1995, Tjioe had been experimenting with the "creation of a global Chinese cooking style that would appeal to any global citizen without adjusting it to suit the local palette." To begin with, he admits, he did not have any great success, but come the millennium, his evolutionary, rather than revolutionary, cuisine began to take off. By 2003, when My Humble House opened, it was skyrocketing. Later ventures in China, Japan and elsewhere have confirmed this is a trend that is here to stay.

Even though the restaurant has a distinctly Asian aesthetic, it is also unashamedly urban, upscale and modern. From the décor to the black-clad waiters to the presentation of the food, the approach is futuristic. At the entrance, huge lilies in glass vases, a small bar and an angular water feature pave the way into the two-level restaurant proper, where modern interpretations of classic Ming furniture, spirals of bright chiffon fabric, a concrete wall with fiber optic "star" lights and granite floors present an interior that

Left Tall order: An oversized chair upholstered in red velvet greets diners at the entrance with a touch of whimsy. Here in the foyer there is no view of the restaurant itself; it is only after you cross the small bridge at right, cooled down psychologically and physically, that the restaurant reveals itself.

Above Black and white is the predominant color scheme at Space@My Humble House, the annex adjacent the restaurant proper. A zen-like Japanese aesthetic permeates throughout with textured screens, dark wood and white furniture.

Below Elongated, high-backed Ming-style chairs made from *zi tan* wood, a rare hardwood from China usually used to make a traditional Chinese musical instrument called the *guzheng*, were handmade in China.

is sensual and sensuous ... and decidedly un-humble. From the tips of its chopsticks to the last sips of its signature green tea cocktail, My Humble House speaks volumes about sophistication.

A 13-seat private dining room raised on massive slabs of white marble with rose-petal lined walls overlooks the kitchen and, next door, a more recent addition is Space@My Humble House. Catering to a more casual clientele, it offers glamorized local favorites such as *char kway teow* using *wagyu* beef instead of cheaper cuts. Designed by Tokyo-based Junpei Yamagiwa, it is a sleek space characterized by private booths with Japanese-inspired screens and a large central communal table with a black pool. Bamboo, planted by Tung Lok outside the floor-to-ceiling windows, completes the scene.

Below East meets West in the tableware selection in the private dining room adjacent the kitchen. Complementing the modern Chinese food, flatware is from Ercuis in the Oise region in France, while china is mainly from Limoges, with some pieces from Japan.

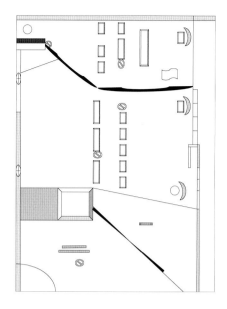

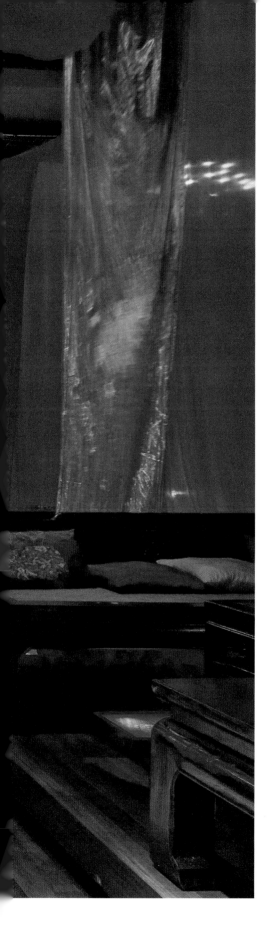

FORBIDDEN CITY

Commodities' trader turned restaurateur, Michael Ma, opened his first bar in 1999 on Singapore's Club Street. Today, there are close to 20 restaurants, bars and clubs operating under his IndoChine trademark, including the one featured on these pages. Bar SáVánh, situated in a shophouse, was difficult to design; the narrow layout of such structures do not accommodate themselves easily to hordes of revelers coming in and out, and bartenders and waiters need sinuosity and virtuosity to avoid the traffic. Nonetheless, it was an overnight success: harking back to his Laotian origins, the Aussie entrepreneur melded Buddha statuary and other Eastern elements with water, Western technology and wit.

This mix has worked well — and most of Ma's subsequent ventures, give or take a little tweaking, are designed along similar, if significantly larger, lines. Forbidden City, a relative newcomer in his ever-expanding empire, was easy to configure in comparison to Bar SáVánh. With the luxury of space and highly individual architecture, it was a case of marrying "cutting-edge technology with ancient artifacts."

Housed in a 150-year-old trader's residence overlooking the Singapore River, the building oozes Oriental glamour. It wasn't like this when Ma acquired it though: The house had been decimated by termites, and reconstruction included the addition of a totally new roof in the ancient style, as well as the installation of reinforced concrete pillars, treated wood installation and more. Some of the old features remain though: the faded flagstones downstairs are originals, as are the elaborate façade and much of the brickwork.

Explains Ma: "When I plan a restaurant or bar, first of all I start with the architecture." In the case of this site, the building's Chinese heritage instigated both the Chinese-themed décor and the neo-classical Chinese cuisine. Pride of place goes to the placement of scores of 1.9-m (6ft, 2 inch) tall terracotta warrior reproductions, sourced in Xian, as well as a host of antiquities: numerous antique panels with gold calligraphy, ancient Buddha statues and other carved wooden artworks. Downstairs, these are accompanied by mauve, pink and gold drapes, a central raised wooden platform with reproduction opium beds for lounging, comfy sofas, intimate seating booths with sexy, silk cushions, and a fashion-forward vibe. New technology, in the form of sound-and-light projections, modernist glass tanks, ubiquitous plasma screens with surfing scenes and a state-of-the-art German-made PSE sound system, complete the sensuous space.

If the club downstairs has the vibe of a Mandarin's manoir, the restaurant above is fit for an Emperor. The gallery feel is furthered and refined in an interior that epitomizes sensory appeal — in the cuisine, the décor and the service. Ma scoured central China for all the tables and chairs, most of them antique, and placed them beneath a soaring, multi-beamed Chinese roof. Floors of highly polished rosewood, a strong blush color scheme on the walls, and double-height concrete columns sheathed in white silk make for an opulent dining experience.

Left Indochine owner Michael Ma describes himself as "experimental," with an interest in antiquities that was picked up when he lived in Australia and his then girlfriend's parents were antique collectors. He designs all his own restaurants, but liaises with sound-and-light technicians and experts, as well as builders and carpenters.

Above Highly polished antique furniture, including this magnificent opium bed, gives the upstairs restaurant a formal feel. Here, the warrior statues are on bended knee, as if in deference to diners.

Left Chinese calligraphy panels and stone statues, as well as antique furniture and furnishings were all sourced in China, giving Forbidden City more than a touch of the exotic East. The figures in foreground are China-made reproductions of ancient Chinese god statues. The pictures on the cabinet behind are of *men shen* or deities that are pasted on the doors of Chinese households to prevent evil influences from entering.

Right The perimeter of one of the downstairs club's dance floors is decked out with low-level loungers, chiffon drapes in hot cerise and elaborate chandeliers. Combined with state-of-the-art LED lighting, it makes for a heady mix.

Above The long bar is the only modernist feature in the restaurant: featuring back lighting and panels with water bubbles, it continues the water theme from downstairs.

Below Two seamless back-lit bars service the club which holds up to 500 people at maximum capacity: glass shelves seem to hang from nothing against the 6-m (20-ft) length of ever-changing backdrop; how this is achieved is Ma's "secret weapon" he says.

Below Key features: In his Wisma Atria restaurant, Ma constructed a 7.6-m (25-ft) alabaster sharing table and in the Waterfront property a chandelier that turned in on itself to look like a lotus is a talking point. At Forbidden City, technological feats include an acrylic-and-glass tank in the center of the glass pyramid-topped court; reinforced with stainless steel, it glows at night and doubles up as an elevated dance floor at some of the group's outrageous costume parties.

Above The exterior of Forbidden City shows the renovated building in all its glory. The forecourt is filled with rows of terracotta warrior replicas while the main entrance features a modernist take on the Chinese screen wall. Passage is impeded by a cleverly illuminated bulletproof fish tank where the emphasis is on the sculptural rocks rather than the lone baby shark within.

Below Elaborate cutlery and hand-fired ceramic crockery, a formality and slickness in the service and the integrity of an interior that is sensitive to site, architecture and cultural history is a welcome relief after the banal plasticity of the S$80 million makeover by CapitaLand, the owners of Clarke Quay.

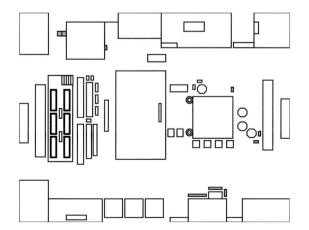

GRAZE

Yenn Wong, creative director and co-owner of Graze, freely admits to falling into the hospitality business by chance. When her father bought a run-down guesthouse for overseas Chinese in Hong Kong and asked her to do something "cool" with it, she obliged by transforming it into the city's first boutique hotel. The coup came in the form of Philippe Starck design, but full credit must also go to the entrepreneur herself. After all, without her at the helm, JIA would never have got off the ground.

The same can be said for Graze, a lifestyle bar/restaurant/lounge that opened in Singapore in April 2006. "Once I started in the hospitality business, I was hooked," she confided from the upstairs balcony of her latest project. Looking down over the expansive garden with angular water feature, casually arranged chairs and tables, and a relaxing lounge area, she allowed herself a smile. Nervous of opening a business on her home turf, she had waited for the right opportunity.

This came in the form of Rochester Park, an area earmarked by the Singapore government as a "lifestyle complex," combining bars and restaurants with galleries, spas and such like. Whether this ambition will ever be fully realized remains to be seen, but the first few venues in the enclave are promising. All are housed in two-storey '40s former homes of British government employees and businessmen and take full advantage of leafy parkland surrounds.

Graze combines the ambience and coziness of an old colonial home with a hip and stylish aesthetic. "The idea is to have different areas with different atmospheres within the whole place," explains Wong. "At the entrance there is a projector and white wall screen within a relaxing outdoor lounge area where we play old black-and-white classic films; then there's the garden with modern wooden pavilions for outdoor dining. As you move into the house, the dining area is very clean and homey, while upstairs there is a fun bar to chill with friends for cocktails."

Graze is all about "eating at a leisurely pace in relaxed surroundings," says Wong. The grassy lawns of the 465-sq-m (5,000 sq-ft) gardens and the fresh, airy ambience were an inspiration for its name, as is the special grazing menu designed for those who prefer to try small portions of a variety of dishes. Whether you opt for the cream-and-chocolate toned bar with its mix of leather and wood or the streamlined dining room or the outdoor woven rattan loungers, the choice is yours. All are very different, but are united by a common "contemporary colonial" atmosphere. From the small details (sweet chandeliers from GEO in trendy H1 in Bangkok) to the wider picture (expansive lawns, careful space planning), Graze is chic, inviting and very much of the here and now.

Right Delineated by a stand of bamboo on one side and the house on the other, the garden is particularly atmospheric at night. Candles seemingly floating on the water feature and ambient lighting cast a romantic glow over the leafy enclave.

Above and opposite bottom Mint condition: The upstairs lounge bar named Mint is the most urban of the spaces in Graze. Mixing leather and wood furniture with white marble topped tables, it features a long outside balcony, a cigar section and a bar. The space is divided by a large organic room divider from Space.

Opposite top The inside dining room on the ground floor features blond wood and metal with exposed concrete floors and walls adorned with a selection of landscape and food related prints. Wire mesh chairs are Eames' repros, while the single-leg tables were custom-made to order in pale wood.

Above The film projection outdoor antechamber as seen from the upstairs balcony. Extensive use of unfinished concrete is used for flooring throughout.

Right Movie night: The vision of Yenn Wong was realized by Melbourne's BURO Architects in association with Hecker Phelan and Guthrie Interiors (HP&G). The group also designed JIA Boutique Hotels' Shanghai property — and Wong has plans for another JIA in Thailand's Krabi too.

Opposite A square bar, clad with glass tiling from Italian mosaic specialists Bisazza in the floral opus romano motif, is contemporary in shape yet rather nostalgic in concept. This is perfectly fitting for the building, as is the Zeppelin pendant lamp in the Cocoon range from Flos above it. Designed by Marcel Wanders, it provides diffused lighting from a ghost-like silhouette.

RANG MAHAL

Princely dining in India brings to mind courtyards beneath the stars, the sounds of trickling water, hand-carved statuary, Rajasthani tents, silks and sirens. All these were the inspiration for the decorative scheme behind Rang Mahal, a modern Indian restaurant in Singapore. Originally operating in the now defunct Imperial Hotel, it is owned and operated by the Jhunjhnuwala family whose company Hind Group has property, development and F & B interests. When the Imperial was demolished, the family decided to resurrect Rang Mahal, its signature restaurant, in a contemporary setting in the Pan Pacific Hotel.

Designed by Wong Chiu Man (now of WarnerWong) and Warren Chen, Rang Mahal is Singaporean-designed but Indian-made. Indian materials predominate — and each and every fixture and fitting was custom crafted in India: woven brass screens, different textures of granite for walls and kitchen counter, scored brass fountains, pillars in a metallic mosaic, ebony tables, a ceiling trellis of simple mahogany and rough teak pillars.

The restaurant has the ability to look both old and new at the same time, a rare quality in any interior. Wong Chiu Man, who was the guiding force behind the conservation project Xin Tian Di in Shanghai, says that the intention was to pay homage to tradition but also to look to the future.

As the Jhunjhnuwala family has a strong base in Hong Kong, they are fervent disciples of feng shui — so the brief was to combine feng shui principles with a modern Indian aesthetic. Built to resemble a courtyard at night, the space is accessed by a wooden bridge that straddles a small pool. Spots and a central dome with sparkling "star-lights" echo a night sky, while mock doors, made from woven brass screens, resemble exits to the exterior. These are set at intervals along stacked granite walls, in front of which are brass water features whose bubbling water sounds mingle with Indian music in a suitably exotic manner.

Left Clad entirely in orange organza, this entrance lounge, used primarily as a cigar and cognac bar, is evocative of north Indian pavilions. The Jhunjhnuwala family's private Ganesh is displayed within a locally made silk and semi-precious stone mesh "frame" designed by Wong Chiu Man.

Above A granite kitchen counter with large copper serving vessels lines one side of Rang Mahal. The restaurant serves modern southern, northern and coastal Indian food.

Right Sheathed in a highly tactile, metallic fabric, the private dining room show-cases two Northern Indian tribal paintings in cow dung with natural inks. Displayed in simple teak and glass frames, they allow diners to appreciate the sparkling fabric behind.

A frieze depicting Indian musicians in sandstone — a sitar, tabla and flute player — runs along one side, while a set of sliding doors leads into a private dining room. This sensuous space is swathed entirely in an amazingly tactile cloth, that is 50 percent silk and 50 percent aluminum. Beneath this metallic canopy is an impressive modular teak table, ideal for occasion dining. Along one side of the room hang two tribal paintings in muted colors.

Throughout, the spirit of India (albeit with a distinctly modern twist) is evoked with an eye for detail, careful maintenance and high-quality materials. Recent additions in the restaurant include ebony tables with a beautiful grain and woven copper central panels, a floral carpet from Thailand and a pavilion-style, organza-clad lounge at the entrance. The fact that Rang Mahal opened in 2000, but looks vibrant and modern today, is testimony to its timeless design.

Top Level crossing: A water feature and "bridge," composed of wooden slats set in a certain direction according to feng shui principles, is flanked by an old Indian millstone on one side and a Ganesh statue on the other. It acts as the de facto entrance to the restaurant where a Satish Gujral sculpture is displayed.

Above Designer Wong Chiu Man, known for F & B and hospitality projects as well as residential ones, combines Indian tradition with a clean-lined modernity in the interior. The outer perimeter, here, is built from stacked granite blocks, in front of which are a series of scored brass water fountains.

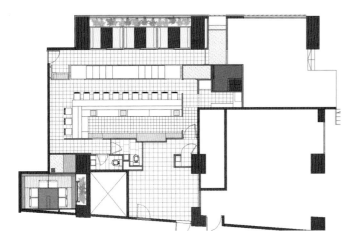

AOKI

From its sleek bronze-and-glass exterior, discreet entrance and an interior that sports a *washi* paper ceiling sculpture, a fake bamboo "mural" and *hinoki* wood sushi counter, Aoki is the epitome of understated sophistication. Light-toned and airy, it is also heavily tactile and highly detailed in both conception and content. Layers of tone and texture are its predominant features.

Owned by Les Amis Group, a restaurant partnership synonymous with fine dining, top of the range wines and exclusivity, Aoki opened in 2003. In keeping with the group's ethos, this is a high-end venue, where top-quality Japanese cuisine is the order of the day and night. This is unsurprising since its director/executive chef Kunio Aoki formerly cooked for Japanese Emperor Akihito in his younger days.

Aoki — and the adjacent Les Amis flagship restaurant — is entirely designed by Japanese interior architect, Koichiro Ikebuchi, of Ikebuchi Atelier. Previously with Super Potato (see pages 98–109) Ikebuchi-san is probably best known for the architecture and interiors of Uma Ubud, a slightly ascetic COMO hotel in Bali. Freely admitting to a partiality for clean lines and simplicity, he says: "At the same time I want some fun touches and some texture."

Aoki has both. Divided into a lower sushi counter area with adjoining tatami room for four, and an upper section that is more modern, the restaurant reveals its layers slowly, almost reluctantly. Entrance is through a hand-woven *noren* curtain, via a volcanic stepping-stone porch — and the first thing one notices in the long, thin, high-ceilinged space is a dramatic installation of hanging strips of hand-made rice-paper, cut and rounded in the shape of a dome. Running the entire length of the restaurant, it is lit from the side and, with the air-conditioning on, the sheets flutter minimally almost like rippling water.

It's aesthetic certainly, yet it also serves to lower the ceiling and delineate the space. On the right are three seating booths for fine dining, in the center a wooden staircase with double partition, and on the left the welcoming sushi counter. Fronted with Hans Wegner rustic chairs and backed by cabinetry fashioned from cedar wood from the Kurobe, this section is the most traditionally Japanese in execution.

The addition of another small private room, and a boudoir-style bar that separates Aoki from Les Amis, ensures that the restaurant is full of surprises. It is almost as if Ikebuchi-san is playing a little game: the sober exterior opens to reveal hidden gems.

Right Separated from the street by an opaque glass double wall that houses fake bamboo which casts shadows and atmosphere, seating booths are intimate and cute. Accessed through *washi*-covered *shouji* (sliding doors), they feature custom-designed brown leather banquettes and a central wooden table.

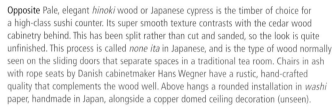

Opposite Pale, elegant *hinoki* wood or Japanese cypress is the timber of choice for a high-class sushi counter. Its super smooth texture contrasts with the cedar wood cabinetry behind. This has been split rather than cut and sanded, so the look is quite unfinished. This process is called *none ita* in Japanese, and is the type of wood normally seen on the sliding doors that separate spaces in a traditional tea room. Chairs in ash with rope seats by Danish cabinetmaker Hans Wegner have a rustic, hand-crafted quality that complements the wood well. Above hangs a rounded installation in *washi* paper, handmade in Japan, alongside a copper domed ceiling decoration (unseen).

Above left Step on it: The central staircase (seen in background) is made from maple with a double partition of blackheart sassafras wood, a hardwood from Tasmania. It has a distinctive grain and a sweet scent. The staircase serves the dual purpose of dividing the restaurant and providing visual appeal.

Above right The bronze-and-glass exterior of Aoki with *noren* curtain "door."

Below A small private dining room for four is made to look larger with a carefully placed wall mirror.

INK CLUB BAR

Designed by Alice Nguyen and Andrew Moore at Hirsch Bedner Associates, Ink Club Bar is an assured mix of leather, luxe and lounging, with a classy refinement in its details. These take the form of silver bead niche dividers, organza and velvet drapes, custom-designed seating and light projected in different forms and colors, as well as a statement-making bar. And that is just the design: a large cigar selection, great drinks, a house band and chill-out vibes, make this a seriously cool venue.

Opened in 2004, the bar is housed in Raffles The Plaza hotel near the Esplanade and Suntec City. On the ground floor, it may be accessed from the hotel lobby or from its own low-key private entrance. Once ensconced inside, the palette is unashamedly sexy: a mix of chrome, black and red. As a blot of ink has no definite shape, but can morph and flow into different forms, so too can the multi-functional space. Fairly open-plan, with a boxy central bar, curtains can be opened or closed and seating moved around to form different booths or conversation niches. Similarly, as the night progresses, state-of the-art pre-programmed lighting by Stephen Gough of Project Lighting Design changes areas into intimate smoochy cubes, or more lively dance sections.

A spacious bar area with a stage for a band, dominated by an enormous custom-designed mirror, comprises the main area. Radiating off this is an adjacent VIP boudoir-boho lounge with one wall entirely clad in red leather; a circular semi-enclosed upper deck; and a wall of silver beads behind which nestle six or so seating clusters for four or more. Grey concrete on floors and grey-sheen hand-troweled Venetian plaster walls present a suitably neutral backdrop for the drama within.

"We play with all five senses at Ink," explains a hotel spokes-person. "In addition to the usual sights, sounds, touch and taste,

Right The black-and-red VIP room features one wall entirely clad in red leather. A low-slung, black leather sofa designed by Francesco Binfaré for Edra with mock-croc cushions is seen in foreground. The carpet, designed by Alice Nguyen to resemble ink smears, adds a luxe touch.

we also pump fragrances into the space through the air-conditioning; this purifies any smell of smoke and also adds different scents to the atmosphere." With your sense of smell catered for, you'll find your hands caressing a faux fur cushion or a velveteen chair, your eyes taking in a futuristic light display, and your taste buds tantalized by top-notch bites and beverages.

This — after all — is a seriously sensuous venue. Says designer Nguyen: "Our aim was to go for a Wow Factor. We designed Ink round the lifestyle of the projected patrons: as they are über-cool, so is their lounge of choice."

Above Custom-crafted rounded sofas in the club continue the black-and-red color scheme. High-gloss lacquered cocktail tables are Asian inspired.

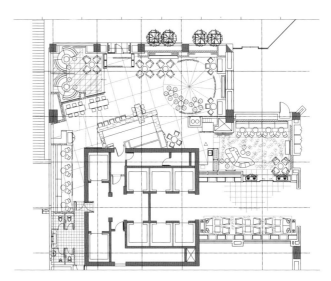

Below Two over-sized Chesterfield-inspired red leather armchairs were custom designed for men who certainly don't eat quiche! Nevertheless, the faux fur black cushions add a feminine touch.

Right top and bottom Custom-crafted chairs come in three types: low round numbers with black wood circular backs, the same but bar-stool height for high tables, and comfy bucket seats for the more horizontally inclined. Poufs are space saving in the club area.

Above Long division: Floor-to-ceiling curtain dividers, made from nickel beads sourced from a US supplier, serve to delineate space, adding privacy to seating areas. Their semi-transparent, textural sheen is glossy and glam.

Left High quality silk curtains are also used as space dividers. On left can be seen the enormous angled mirror that serves to enlarge the space.

Opposite Men only? The masculine bar, with black granite top, is softened with an out-jutting section made from shiny acrylic from Australia. This is curved under at the end using a heat-bending process; the shape is echoed in the aluminum shelving behind.

UPPER CLUB

In a bid to up the ante in Singapore's somewhat sedate dining scene, the management at CHIJMES, an entertainment, retail and dining hub set in the confines of an old colonial enclave, hit on the concept of a supper club with dancing. But not any old dancing, you understand. No, this was to be an up market center for the rhumba, the cha cha cha, the waltz, foxtrot, even a tango or two. With a resident orchestra and a sprung dance floor. With fine dining — and atmosphere, panache, pizzazz.

"The idea behind Upper Club was to bring back some glamour into Singapore's supper scene," says Esther Yong, one of the Directors of CHIJMES. She saw a gap in the market, and felt that CHIJMES, with its neo-gothic and neoclassical buildings, cloistered walls and long walkways, would serve as an ideal setting for such a venture. Securing a large, upper-storey hall with views over the central courtyard set the scheme in motion.

Erik L'Heureux, an architect and interior designer based in New York but with some experience in Asia, was enlisted to put her vision into reality. Certainly, the beautifully proportioned hall with filigree-ed ceiling, elegant pillars and generous windows was a fine starting point. But, the intention wasn't to hark back to the past, but to look forward with a new and appealing design.

"The main conundrum of designing Upper Club was how to combine the new with the old," explains L'Heureux. "How could the historical legacy of the architecture of CHIJMES be combined with something new and different?" This, of course, was also the dichotomy of the concept: how to present the Old World glamour of ballroom dancing in a fresh, rather than a staid, way?

The solution came in the form of a "hybrid," specifically employing a type of wood-paneled "skin" that is separated from the historic context of CHIJMES as it is literally pulled away from the existing walls and plaster. Warm, rich Indian rosewood square

Right Dancing for dinner: The voluminous hall features a custom-built sprung dance floor in Brazilian cherry wood, while the ceiling montage is a direct play on the curtains at the famous Four Seasons Restaurant in New York designed by Mies van der Rohe. The lighting is adjustable and can reflect off the 7,450 swaying shards in any color.

Above An imposing entrance chamber is austere and calm, belying the experience of entering the club afterwards.

Right top The designer, Erik l'Heureux of 212box, a New York-based firm, describes the restaurant, bar and dance floor as "compositions of architectural 'dresses' suspended from the existing structure of CHIJMES." This close-up of the ceiling is one of the "dresses" L'Heureux refers to.

Right below Placed beneath Czechoslovakian chandeliers, sourced from Le Merciers locally in Singapore, are pristine seating clusters. Chairs, custom crafted in Malaysia based on a classic Louis XIV design, are made contemporary with white millwork.

panels are used, furthering the illusion that they have been almost temporarily "stuck" there. At the bottom they curve slightly — either into in-built sofa seating that juts out from the wall, or next to the floor where the panels are backlit.

The overall illusion is an encased box, with a 111 sq-m (1,200 sq-ft) central dance floor, stage at the far end for an orchestra, and elegant cream-dressed tables and chairs all around. Above the tables are romantic crystal chandeliers and, above the dancers, a ceiling installation comprising a mass of suspended custom brushed and chromed aluminum blades. Set into motion with precisely calibrated air-conditioning, they change color with the lighting and sway and sashay above twirling couples beneath. If that doesn't make the heart flutter, I don't know what will.

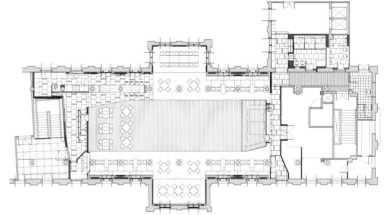

Above The bar is one continuous linear construction, going from the floor up to the length of the bar itself, then ending in a u-shape that houses a large vase for grandiose floral displays. Made from botticino classico marble from Italy, it has double sided seating in comfy bucket-style high chairs.

ZUMA GRILL & BAR

In 2005 and 2006, CapitaLand, owners of Clarke Quay, invested S$80 million to revamp a stretch of riverside heritage architecture that once comprised godowns, merchants' houses and offices, and traders' shophouses. Part of the government's drive to revitalize the Singapore River into a new millennium entertainment and leisure complex, Clarke Quay's new incarnation has had a mixed reaction from the public.

Certainly, the shabby warehouse-style shops, stalls and coffee shops have gone for good. In their place are spanking new restaurants, bars and nightclubs; a Crazy Horse theater; a reverse bungy jump and a Disney-style adventure ride. Garish mock "lily pads" line the waterfront, almost obscuring the river itself, and high canopy polymer roofing and cooling technology keep the tropical heat and rain at bay. While some of this is undoubtedly commendable, some is unfortunately misconceived, even downright ugly.

What isn't ugly, however, is one of the new kids on the block, ultra-chic Zuma Grill & Bar. With both al-fresco and indoor dining and drinking, it is a compact design that utilizes fully the somewhat small plot. Designers Alice Nguyen and Andrew Linwood have gone to some lengths to preserve the original architectural shell of the building, and the façade, with symmetric shutters and original pillars, faces the river in a cool grey palette. Inside, an asymmetric entrance pathway in sandstone and oblique timber ceiling panels distance the interior from the rigidity of the square godown architecture. It's easy on the eye, both inside and out.

"The main entrance is accentuated with a bold brushed bronze portal," explains Nguyen, "and once inside, a romantic glow of golden hues is reflected from gorgeous antique smoked mirror panels, iridescent amber bulb-pendants overhead, and warm waves of natural sandstone underfoot." Seating is on the left, the bar ahead, and natural oak and antique mirror panels clad the wall

Right The interiors at Zuma are very calming, with a modern vibe that suits the music and munching on offer. Generous windows in the glass-roofed dining area are sheathed in sheer linen, giving diners a feel for what is outside, yet protecting them from outsiders. Materials were chosen carefully too: High quality timbers, dangling metal light shades, bronze sculptures and antique mirrors all create a warm ambience.

on the right. Clean lines characterize custom-crafted furniture and upholstery is a smart combo of broad loop slate grey on the backs of chairs and thinly striped mustard yellow on seats and fronts. A selection of bronze sculptures and z-formation bronze occasional high tables adjacent structural pillars are classy additions.

There are two bars, one outside beneath a canopy, and one inside the restaurant. They are identical and incorporate layers of natural oak and wenge timber panels and antique mirror on fronts, and white carrera marble on tops. "The bar front is a play of lines and planes," explains Nguyen. It formed the inspiration for Zuma's elegant signage, but this is also reflected in the louvered shutters of the exterior. As with all good design, Zuma's sum is made up of its many coherent and corresponding parts.

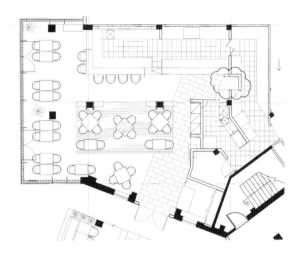

Opposite The outdoor bar mirrors the one inside.

Above The pièce de la résistance of the restaurant entrance is the use of antique mirror panels from Schott. They provide warm finishing, an ultra-smooth texture and a visually appealing glow.

Above Logos and branding being buzzwords of all cool companies, Zuma has a suitably exotic name. Its signage is echoed in the clean lines of the bar front panels, the louvered shutters of the building and the clean lines of the design.

Above High tables: "The z-formation bronze uprights at the drinking ledges play off the Zuma name while showing a splash of whimsical detail," says Nguyen.

DESIGNER BIOGRAPHIES

212box
A New York City architecture and design partnership formed by Eric Clough, Erik L'Hereux and Heather Benski in 1999, 212box focuses on residential, commercial and retail architecture, large-scale public projects, urban design, product design, graphics, advertising and film. Architectural rigor is combined with branding, graphic identities and promotion from planning stage through to advertising and completion.

a2jdesign
Comprising three partners (Ary Juwono, Ijus Julius Susanto and Adelinah Chandrarahardja), this interior design house specializes in retail, residential and hospitality projects in Indonesia. Jakarta-based, the trio are known for their innovative, fun and alternative designs. They are proud of being local to Indonesia, but with an international design aesthetic. As they say: "A2J style is East meets West!"

ArchiCentre Sdn Bhd
ArchiCentre was established in Kuala Lumpur in 1994 and is run by Dr Tan Loke Mun and Lim Wei Hong. The firm's work embraces and interprets regionalism in a modern context, and it is the recipient of many architectural awards. In a rapidly changing world landscape, ArchiCentre seeks to find a balance between the rush towards modern standardization and the well designed, highly individual building.

Axis.Point Design
Describing itself as a one-stop shop from design to submissions to project management, Axis.Point Design is a Singapore-based multi-disciplinary design practice established in 1995. The design principal is Song-Por Tan, trained in architecture in the UK. The office has extensive experience in retail, office, entertainment, F & B and private residences. Its holistic approach to design seeks to enliven the built environment with design approaches embracing culture, climate and suitable technology.

Ou Baholyodhin
Anglo-Thai, Ou Baholyodhin began his career as a furniture and product designer, but has since become very well known for his interior design projects as well. Working out of a studio in London, he brings a unique East-West approach to residential, hospitality and retail projects. Most of his spaces are characterized by a calm, serene sophistication and many of his unusual furniture pieces are already collectors' items.

Tony Chi & Associates
Established in 1984, Tony Chi & Associates is a multi-disciplinary design firm engaged in planning and consulting, the development and execution of architectural, interior and landscape design, and urban planning. Particularly famous for theatrical restaurant designs with an emphasis on color, texture and a mix of elements, Chi is US-based but undertakes a number of international projects.

Design Spirits Co Ltd
The brainchild of interior designer Yuhkichi Kawai, Tokyo-based Design Spirits is a relatively young company with a youthful, exuberant style. Using the "spirit of craftsmanship" and an "earnest attitude," its aim is to create spaces that have both longevity and spirit. It received many awards for its groundbreaking designs at Starhill Gallery, Kuala Lumpur.

dwp cityspace
The Thai arm of design worldwide partnership, a collection of individually owned businesses in Asia Pacific, dwp cityspace is known in Bangkok for its residential and hospitality projects. All the dwp companies share a consistent design philosophy that is centered on dynamic collaboration between firms. This integrated design system is a unique and successful approach to delivering architectural and interior design solutions.

Espace Concept
Under the guidance of Fredo Taffin, Espace Concept is an architecture and interior design firm with offices in Australia and Bali. Known for cutting-edge tropical modern designs that combine Western know-how and clean lines with extensive use of local materials and craftspeople, Espace Concept is well known for its tropical-modern private residences, villas and hotels in Asia and beyond.

Hecker Phelan & Guthrie Interiors
HP&G is a Melbourne-based interior design team that specializes in hospitality interiors. Often working with BURO architects, it collaborated on Yenn Wong's JIA hotel in Hong Kong, and more recently Singapore's Graze restaurant, featured in this book. The firm's signature can be seen on some notable restaurants in several Australian cities: Reserve and all the restaurants, including est, in the Establishment Hotel in Sydney.

Hirsch Bedner Associates
A leader in hospitality interior design worldwide, HBA has offices from Atlanta to Shanghai, Los Angeles to London. "Our ultimate objective is to add value, to raise standards and enhance the brand of a project's owner and operator," it profers. Providing a comprehensive package of design services from planning to installation, it also has a graphic design division that offers brand and identity programming.

Atelier Ikebuchi
Koichiro Ikebuchi, an interior architect previously with Japan über-firm Super Potato, founded Atelier Ikebuchi in Singapore. Specializing in both interiors and architecture, it is probably most well known for the interior design of the slightly ascetic Uma Ubud hotel in Bali. Atelier Ikebuchi's portfolio includes residences in Hong Kong and the Middle East, product and lighting design in Japan, as well as hospitality projects in Southeast Asia.

Jaya & Associates
Set up in 1993 by designers Jaya Ibrahim and John Saunders, Jaya & Associates is well known globally for its super luxurious, tactile designs and a strong sense of place. Interiors always use very high-quality materials and are lavish in scale and execution. Often providing a contemporary reinterpretation of the past, Jaya's projects are instantly recognizable (although by no means uniform).

Antony Liu
Most well known as the architect of the uber-cool design hotel The Balé in Bali, Liu is a Jakarta-based interior designer and architect. With countless residential and hospitality projects under his belt, he is known for his hip, sleek and modern designs.

Ministry of Design
Ministry of Design is an award winning spatial design practice that seeks to disturb, question and redefine the fundamental elements of Space, Ritual and Perception. Led by architecturally trained design director Colin Seah, the firm undertakes hospitality, retail and residential work. Award winning projects include Hu'u Bar, Bangkok and the New Majestic Hotel, Singapore.

Nexus Design
Set up by Indonesian architect Shinta Siregar who graduated from the Royal Melbourne Institute of Technology in 1988, Nexus is a small design studio based in Bali. Siregar has worked on a number of General Hotel Management projects, as well as other projects in the hospitality field. She was the architect on the Club at the Legian project.

Alice Nguyen
Formerly with HBA, Los Angeles, Alice Nguyen has a small design consultancy in Southeast Asia. Specializing

in both residential and hospitality interior design mainly in Singapore and Jakarta, Nguyen is known for her imaginative use of materials, crafty space planning and modernist eye.

Orbit Design Studio

With offices in Bangkok, Tokyo and London, multi-disciplinary firm Orbit is increasingly recognized for its innovative and contemporary design solutions. Using high-tech computer graphic visualization, it offers high-quality rendered artwork as well as completed projects that offer a unified design identity.

Poole Associates

With Managing Director Ed Poole, an American architect, at the helm, Singapore-based Poole Associates has gone from strength to strength. Offering a one-stop service in architecture, interiors, lighting and animation, the firm has designed numerous spaces in the hospitality, office, residential and retail fields. "We do not adhere to a particular design style," the partners assert. "Final solutions evolve from the many factors relating to a project, each viewed from a fresh perspective."

Imaad Rahmouni

Algiers-born Imaad Rahmouni cut his design teeth collaborating with Philippe Starck — and has since gone on to become one of Paris' most sought-after interior architects. His signature neo-modern style varies from airy elegance to theatrical opulence, and all his projects have undeniable cachet. High profile clients include restaurateurs such as the Pourcel brothers and Cathy and David Guetta, and French automobile makers Renault.

Sardjono Sani

Based in Indonesia, Sardjono Sani is a modernist architect with over 20 years experience. He took his Masters degree in architecture in 1990 at the University of Colorado and is currently director and principal architectural designer of PT Bias Tekno-Art Kreasindo. Having designed numerous malls, offices, residences and retail spaces, he attempted to get away from "the traditional hospitality model" at his own hotel Kemang Icon. Ideally, he prefers an experimental approach in both architecture and interior design projects.

Richard Sea

Even though Sea trained in Communications, his first foray into architecture was the design and building of his Bali dream house in 2002. He then designed The GreenHouse, a modernist restaurant in Ubud, and has since relocated to Singapore. However, he travels back to the island of the gods regularly to offer design, marketing and PR consultancy to clients in the hospitality and retail business there.

Design Studio SPIN

Set up by ex-Super Potato designer Yasuhiro Koichi, this Tokyo-based firm has designed many notable food and beverage venues in Asia. The unique SPIN identity has been achieved by combining Asian motifs, materials and colors with cutting-edge lighting technology and clean lines. Nevertheless, no two projects look alike.

Super Potato

Based in Tokyo, Super Potato is an international interior design firm led by Takashi Sugimoto. Known for its revolutionary restaurant and bar design, it aims to create spaces that give an overall experience as well as a pretty picture. Super Potato undertakes a broad range of commercial projects mainly in the retail and hospitality industries — and designs are invariably high quality, textural and modern. It is generally recognized as having invented the multi-kitchen, multi-dining space restaurant.

Aamer Taher Design Studio

ATDS was established in 1994 by Aamer Taher two years after he returned to Singapore from London where he trained in the Architectural Association School of Architecture. An architect and an artist, Taher specializes in translating the narrative of the brief into built form: architecture, interiors and landscaping are all designed under one roof with a thorough understanding of function, culture, climate and context.

Koji Takeda & Associates

Tokyo-based Takeda is at the helm of Koji Takeda and Associates, the firm behind the super-cool Martini Bar and Dava restaurant at the Ritz-Carlton Resort in Jimbaran, Bali. Other projects include urban planning and hospitality projects.

Tihany Design

Set up in New York in 1978 by architect and designer Adam D Tihany, Tihany Design is a multi-disciplinary design atelier that concentrates on hospitality design. With an international clientele and a multicultural staff, Tihany Design projects are known for their bold, contemporary designs, their use of color and a highly individual identity.

Calvin Tsao

A founding partner of New York-based Tsao & McKown Architects, Calvin Tsao has a broad range of design experience in international and domestic projects. Be it a small or large commercial or residential development, his work has won numerous international awards. Tsao is also known for his design and art direction of film, dance and theatrical productions and has served as the Eliot Noyes Visiting Design Critic in Architecture at Harvard University.

WarnerWong Pte Ltd

Set up in 2000 by architects Wong Chiu Man and Maria Warner Wong, this Singapore-based company is an international multi-disciplinary design consultancy. Providing master planning, urban, interior and landscape design services throughout Asia, projects vary from a futuristic hotel in India to the restoration of an entire neighborhood of 1900s *shikumen* tenement buildings in Shanghai.

Mada Wijaya

A long-term resident in Bali, Wijaya's main focus is on landscape design. However, he also designs and retails furniture and lamps amongst other items, and turns his hand to architecture and interior design. Architectural projects include his on-going atelier home in Sanur and Taman Bebek, a luxury villa hotel in Ubud.

Wilson & Associates

Specializing in interior architectural design, Wilson & Associates was founded in 1975 by Trisha Wilson, and today has offices in Dallas, New York, Los Angeles, Singapore, Johannesburg and Shanghai. The internationally acclaimed firm specializes in interiors for hotels, restaurants, clubs and casinos. Designers are always encouraged to incorporate a geographical flavor into each project with the use of local craftsmen, artisans and artists — and the firm has received many awards for both new construction and historical renovation.

DESIGNER ADDRESSES

212box LLC
128 Chambers St, Floor 2,
New York, NY 10007, USA
Tel: +1 212 233 9170
www.212box.com

a2jdesign
Jalan Asem 11 No 15A,
Jakarta Selatan, Indonesia
Tel: +61 21 7590 5311
www.a2jdesign.com

Agence Imaad Rahmouni
8 Passage de la Bonne Graine,
75017 Paris, France
Tel: +33 1 40 21 01 05
www.imaadrahmouni.com

ArchiCentre Sdn Bhd
No 33B Jalan SS 15/4E,
47500 Subang Jaya,
Selangor Darul Ehsan, Malaysia
Tel +60 3 5635 2455

Axis.Point Design Pte Ltd
531 Upper Cross Street #03–63,
Singapore 050531
Tel: +65 6533 0112
www.axisptdesign.com

Ou Baholyodhin Studio
Unit 2C, 9–15 Elthorne Road,
London N19 6AJ, UK
Tel: +44 20 7272 2272
www.ou-b.com

Tony Chi & Associates
20 West 36th Street, 9th floor,
New York, NY 10018, USA
Tel: +1 212 868 8686
www.tonychi.com

Design Spirits Co Ltd
2–18–2–202 Ohara Setagaya,
Tokyo 156–0041, Japan
+81 3 3324 9901
www.design-spirits.com

dwp cityspace Ltd
The Dusit Thani Building, Level 11, 946
Rama IV Rd, Bangkok 10500, Thailand
Tel: +66 2267 3939
www.dwpartnership.com

Espace Concept
www.espaceconcept.net

HBA/Hirsch Bedner Associates
170 Bukit Timah Road,
#03–1 Genesis Building,
Singapore 229847
Tel: +65 6337 2511
www.hbadesign.com

Atelier Ikebuchi
www.ikebuchi.com

Jaya & Associates
Jalan Erlangga V No 18,
Jakarta 12110, Indonesia
Tel: +62 21 7279 2107

Ministry of Design
23B Teo Hong Road,
Singapore 088332
Tel: +65 6221 3559
www.modonline.com

Nexus Studio Architects
Perkantoran Duta Wijaya,
Jalan Raya Puputan,
Denpasar, Bali, Indonesia
Tel: +62 361 264 136
www.nexusbali.com

Alice Nguyen
www.maisonid.com

Orbit Design Studio
Unit 2701A, 27th floor, M Thai Tower,
All Seasons Place, 87 Wireless Road,
Bangkok 10330, Thailand
Tel: +66 2 654 3667–9
www.orbitdesignstudio.com

Poole Associates Pte Ltd
Penthouse One, 37th floor, One
Pearlbank, Singapore 169016
Tel: +65 6536 3928
www.poole-associates.com

Design Studio SPIN
Luceria–OB 2–13–21,
Tomigaya Shibuya-ku,
Tokyo 151–0063, Japan
Tel: +81 3 6407 2055
www.ds-spin.com

Super Potato Co Ltd
3–34–17 Kamikitazawa,
Setagayaku, Tokyo 156–0057, Japan
Tel: +81 3 3290 0195
www.superpotato.jp

Aamer Taher Design Studio
25 Jalan Kuning, Singapore 278170
Tel: +65 6476 6441
www.aamertaher.com

Koji Takeda Architects & Associates
Minamiazabu bldg. 4F, 2–13–12,
Minamiazabu, Minato-ku, Tokyo, Japan

Tihany Design
135 West 27th Street, 9th Floor,
New York, NY 10001, USA
Tel: +1 212 366 5544
www.tihanydesign.com

Calvin Tsao
www.tsao-mckown.com

WarnerWong Pte Ltd
30 Hill Street, 01–04, Singapore 179360
Tel: +65 6333 3312
www.warnerwong.com

PT Wijaya Tribwana International
Jalan By Pass Ngurah Rai No 772,
Denpasar, Bali, Indonesia
Tel: +62 361 728 488
www.ptwijaya.com

Wilson & Associates
3 Anson Road #25–00, Springleaf Tower,
Singapore 079909
Tel: + 65 6327 5787
www.wilsonassoc.com

RESTAURANT ADDRESSES

BALI

Dava & Martini Club
The Ritz-Carlton Bali Resort & Spa,
Jalan Karang Mas Sejahtera, Jimbaran,
Bali 80364
Tel: +62 361 702 222
www.ritzcarlton.com

The Club at the Legian
Jalan Laksmana, Seminyak, Bali 80361
Tel: +62 361 730 622
www.ghmhotels.com

Ku De Ta
Jalan Laksmana 9, Seminyak, Bali 80361
Tel: +62 361 736 969
www.kudeta.net

Lamak
Monkey Forest Road, Ubud, Bali
Tel: +62 361 974 668
www.lamakbali.com

Spice
Conrad Bali Resort & Spa,
Jalan Pratama 168, Tanjung Benoa,
Bali 80363
Tel: +62 361 778 788
www.ConradHotels.com

The Wave
Jalan Pantai Kuta 1, Kuta, Bali 80361
Tel: +62 361 760 068
www.wave-kuta.com

The GreenHouse
Pertiwi Resort & Spa, Monkey Forest
Road, Ubud, Bali
Tel: +62 361 978 189

BANGKOK

Bed Supperclub
26 Soi Sukhumvit 11,
Sukhumvit Road, Kloengtoey-nua,
Wattana, Bangkok 10110
Tel: +66 2651 3537
www.bedsupperclub.com

D'Sens
The Dusit Thani, Bangkok,
22nd floor, 946 Rama IV Road,
Bangkok 10500
Tel: +66 2200 9000 ext 2499
www.dusit.com

The Erawan Tea Room
Grand Hyatt Erawan Bangkok,
Erawan Hyatt Mall, 2nd floor,
494 Rajdamri Road, Bangkok 10330
Tel: +66 2254 1234
www.bangkok.grand.hyatt.com

The Dome at State Tower
65th Floor, State Tower Bangkok,
1065 Silom Road, Bangrak,
Bangkok 10500
Tel: +66 2624 9555
www.thedomebkk.com

Drinking Tea Eating Rice and 87+
Conrad Bangkok, All Seasons Place,
87 Wireless Road, Bangkok 10330
Tel: +66 2690 9999
www.ConradHotels.com

Hu'u Bar & Restaurant
Levels 1 & 2, The Ascott Sathorn,
187 South Sathorn Road, Yannawa,
Bangkok 10120
Tel: +66 2676 6673
www.huuinasia.com

SynBar
Nai Lert Park Hotel, 2 Wireless Road,
Bangkok 10330
Tel: +66 2253 0123
www.nailertpark.swissotel.com

Thompson Bar & Restaurant
Jim Thompson Museum House,
6/1 Soi Kasemsan 2, Rama 1 Road,
Bangkok 10330
Tel: +66 2612 3601
www.jimthompson.com

JAKARTA

burgundy and C's
Grand Hyatt Jakarta,
Jalan M. H. Thamrin, Kav. 28–30,
Jakarta 10230
Tel: +61 21 390 1234
www.jakarta.grand.hyatt.com

Cilantro
Kota BNI, Jalan Jend. Sudirman Kav.1,
Jakarta 10220
Tel: +62 21 251 2822

Dragonfly
Graha BIP, Jalan Gatot Subroto 23,
Jakarta 12930
Tel: +62 21 520 6789
www.the-dragonfly.com

The Edge
Kemang Icon, Kemang Raya 1,
Jakarta 12730
Tel: +62 21 719 7989
www.kemangicon.com

Lara Djonggrang & La Bihzad Bar
Jalan Cik Di Tiro 4, Menteng, Jakarta
Tel: +62 21 315 3252
www.tuguhotels.com

The Nine Muses Club
Jalan Wijaya 1 No 25, Kebayoran Baru,
Jakarta 12170
Tel: +62 21 722 1188
www.ninemusesclub.com

XLounge Charcoal Vertigo
Gedung Veteran 16–17th floors,
Plaza Semanggi, Jalan Jend. Sudirman
Kav. 50, Jakarta 12930
Tel: +62 21 2553 9892

KUALA LUMPUR

The Dining Room & Bar
Carcosa Seri Negara,
Taman Tasik Perdan, Persiaran
Mahameru, 50480 Kuala Lumpur
Tel: +60 3 2282 1888
www.ghmhotels.com

EEST
The Westin Kuala Lumpur,
199 Jalan Bukit Bintang,
55100 Kuala Lumpur
Tel: +60 3 2731 8333
www.westin.com/kualalumpur

Feast Village, Gonbei and Tiffin Room
Starhill Gallery, 181 Jalan Bukit Bintang,
55100 Kuala Lumpur
Tel: +60 3 2782 3855
www.starhillgallery.com

sevenatenine
The Ascott Kuala Lumpur
9 Jalan Pinang, 50450 Kuala Lumpur
Tel: +60 3 21617 789
www.sevenatenine.com

SINGAPORE

Aoki
17 Shaw Centre,
1 Scotts Road,
Singapore 228208
Tel: +65 6333 8015
www.lesamis.com.sg

Bold
The Scarlet Hotel,
33 Erskine Road,
Singapore 069333
Tel: +65 6511 3333
www.thescarlethotel.com

The Butter Factory
48 Robertson Quay #01-03,
Riverside 48,
Singapore 238237
Tel: +65 6333 8243
www.thebutterfactory.com

China One
Block 3E River Valley Road,
#02-01, Clarke Quay,
Singapore 179024
Tel: +65 6339 0280
www.baize.com.sg

The Cliff
The Sentosa Resort & Spa,
2 Bukit Manis Road, Sentosa,
Singapore 099891
Tel: +65 6275 0331
www.thesentosa.com

Crystal Jade Golden Palace
290 Orchard Road,
#05-22/24 The Paragon,
Singapore 238859
Tel: +65 6734 6866
www.crystaljade.com

Forbidden City
3A Merchant's Court,
River Valley Road #01-02,
Singapore 179020
Madame Butterfly Tel: +65 6557 6266
Cocoon Tel: +65 6557 62648

Graze
4 Rochester Park,
Singapore 139215
Tel: +65 6775 9000

P S Cafe
28B Harding Road,
Singapore 249549
Tel: +65 6479 3343
www.projectshop.com

Ink Club Bar
Raffles the Plaza,
80 Bras Basah Road,
Singapore 189560
Tel: +65 6431 5581
www.inkclubbar.com

The Line
Shangri-La Hotel,
Orange Grove Road,
Singapore 258350
Tel: +65 6213 4275
www.shangri-la.com

My Humble House
The Esplanade Theatres on the Bay,
#02–27/29 Esplanade Mall,
8 Raffles Avenue, Singapore 039802
Tel: +65 6423 1881
www.tunglok.com

Rang Mahal
Pan Pacific Singapore , Level 3,
7 Raffles Boulevard, Marina Square,
Singapore 039595
Tel: +65 6333 1788
www.rangmahal.com.sg

Upper Club
CHIJMES, 30 Victoria Street #02–01A,
Singapore 187996.
Tel: +65 6338 1313
www.upperclub.com.sg

Zuma Bar & Grill
3C River Valley Road,
#01–01 Clarke Quay,
Singapore 179022
Tel: +65 6339 6797
wwwzumabarandgrill.com

ACKNOWLEDGMENTS

The author and photographer would like to thank the following people for their help, time and commitment during the process of making this book:

Designers
Alice D Nguyen; Ed Poole of Poole Associates; Jaya Ibrahim; Wong Chiu Man, Warren Liu, James Tan, Melissa Ang of Warner Wong; Yuhkichi Kawai of Design Spirits; Koichiro Ikebuchi of Atelier Ikebuchi; Yasuhiro Koichi and Kiyomi Matsuda of Spin Design; Adam D Tihany of Tihany Design; Erik L'Heureux of 212box; Scott Whittaker and Apisake Painupong of dwp cityspace; Imaad Rahmouni; Colin Seah of Ministry of Design; Calvin Tsao of Tsao & McKown Architects; Ou Baholyodhin; Tony Chi of Tony Chi & Associates; Richard Sea; Made Wijaya; Shinta Siregar of Nexus; Dr Tan Loke Mun and Lim Wei Hong of ArchiCentre Sdn Bhd; Sunny Sutanto; Are, Ade and Julius of a2j; Sardjono Sani of Bias Tekno-Art Kreasindo; Antony Liu; Norihiko Shinya of Super Potato; Aamer Taher of Aamer Taher Design Studios.

Properties
Kuala Lumpur: Michele Kwok and the team from Souled Out; Ang Lay Ling and Larry Van Ooyen at Carcosa Seri Negara; Tiang LiMing and Martin B Jones at The Westin; Danielle Pearce and Steffanie Chua at YTL Properties.

Singapore: Kunio Aoki of Aoki; Raymond Lim of Les Amis; Carolyn Tan and Andrew Tjioe of Tung Lok Restaurants Ltd; S Venkat N Reddy and the Jhunjhnuwala family of Rang Mahal; Joleena Seah and Joanna Huang of Shangri-La; Belladonnah Lim of Raffles The Plaza; Michael Ma of IndoChine; Michael Tan of Grace International; Mitchell Noble of Zuma; Serene Lai of China One; Han-Yong Li Lan and Esther Yong of CHIJMES; Marine Tan of Crystal Jade Culinary Concepts Holding; Geri Lee of Sentosa Resort & Spa; Philip Chin, Peter Teo and Richard Chamberlain at PS Café; Bobby Luo of The Butter Factory; Yenn Wong of Graze.

Bangkok: William M Booth of the James H W Thompson Foundation; Harris Kurthip of Nai Lert Park Hotel; Chris Conway, Sammy Carolus and Pathira Nakngam Riley of Grand Hyatt Erawan Bangkok; Wannapa Rakkeo of Conrad Bangkok; Lalana Santos and Sommai Yocapajorn of the Dusit Thani; Terence Tan of Hu'u Bar; Deepak Ohri and Savinee Asavanuchit of the Dome Complex; Sanya Souvanna Phouma and assorted "Bed Mates" at Bed Supperclub.

Bali: Prami Pratiwi, Paul Czuba and Meutia Irataliana of the Ritz-Carlton Bali Resort & Spa; Ruth Zukerman of Conrad Bali Resort & Spa; Dewa Gede Putra Arimbawa of GreenHouse; Arthur Chondros of Ku De Ta; Mr and Mrs Malik and Roland Lickert of Lamak; Hansjoerg Meier of the Legian Bali; Kryn Wolszczak of The Wave.

Jakarta: Peter Stettler, Gina Desmeralda and Arifin Darmawan of Grand Hyatt Jakarta; Anhar Setjadibrata, Annette Anhar and Michael Oei of Lara Djonggrang and Dapur Babah; Gil D'Harcour and Buyung Rusmanto of the Nine Muses Club; Christian Rijanto and Kiki Utara of Dragonfly; Frederic F Simon, Joyce Tan and Ronnie of Alila Hotels and Resorts; Felix Denanta of XLounge; Andrew Nugroho and Yuli Widjaja of Cilantro.

Others: Bayu Wibisono and Teresa of Java Books; William Atyeo; Kevin, Tanis and Max McGrath; Yazer Aziz; Gillian Beal; Evelyn Gamueda.

Published by Periplus Editions (HK) Ltd., with editorial offices at 130 Joo Seng Road #06-01, Singapore 368357.

Photographs © 2007 Masano Kawana
Text © 2007 Kim Inglis

ISBN-10: 0-7946-0407-2
ISBN-13: 978-0-7946-0407-3

Distributed by

North America, Latin America & Europe
Tuttle Publishing
364 Innovation Drive
North Clarendon, VT 05759-9436 U.S.A.
Tel: 1 (802) 773-8930
Fax: 1 (802) 773-6993
info@tuttlepublishing.com
www.tuttlepublishing.com

Japan
Tuttle Publishing
Yaekari Building, 3rd Floor
5-4-12 Osaki
Shinagawa-ku
Tokyo 141-0032
Tel: (81) 03 5437-0171
Fax: (81) 03 5437-0755
tuttle-sales@gol.com

Asia Pacific
Berkeley Books Pte. Ltd.
130 Joo Seng Road #06-01
Singapore 368357
Tel: (65) 6280-1330
Fax: (65) 6280-6290
inquiries@periplus.com.sg
www.periplus.com

10 09 08 07
6 5 4 3 2 1

Printed in Singapore